Beneath the

While every precaution has been taken in the preparation of this book, the publisher assumes no responsibility for errors or omissions, or for damages resulting from the use of the information contained herein.

BENEATH THE EPIDEMIC

First edition. October 31, 2024.

Copyright © 2024 Kaitlyn Doht.

ISBN: 979-8227308887

Written by Kaitlyn Doht.

Table of Contents

Introduction 1
The Roots of the Crisis 9
The Cartel Connection 27
The Rise of Fentanyl and Synthetic Drugs 51
Commonly Abused Drugs and Their Impact 65
The Overdose Crisis 77
Crime and Drug-Related Criminal Behavior 87
The Social Cost: Impact on Communities and Families 93
Recovery, Rehabilitation, and Treatment 105
Government and Public Health Responses 125
Looking Forward – Solutions and Hope 137
Final Reflections 149
References and Resources 151

Introduction

The drug crisis in the United States has escalated over recent decades, transforming from a public health concern into a full-blown epidemic. Across communities, addiction devastates families, strains healthcare systems, overwhelms law enforcement, and consumes billions in economic costs. Once isolated to specific regions or demographics, substance abuse now permeates every corner of society, affecting people from all backgrounds. As drugs have evolved in potency and availability, addiction has grown in complexity and impact, creating a network of issues that reach far beyond individual users.

Drug cartels play a central role in fueling America's addiction crisis. Cartels from Mexico and South America, such as the Sinaloa and Jalisco New Generation cartels, control a significant portion of the illegal drug trade in the United States. These organizations function like complex corporations, coordinating networks for production, distribution, and marketing to meet America's seemingly insatiable demand for narcotics. By using well-established smuggling routes and exploiting gaps in border security, they manage to transport massive quantities of drugs into the U.S. every year. Advanced logistics, bribery, and violence enable these cartels to maintain their dominance and evade law enforcement, making them formidable adversaries for U.S. authorities.

Fentanyl and other synthetic opioids have transformed the nature of the drug epidemic. Originally developed as a painkiller, fentanyl is up to 100 times stronger than morphine, and it's frequently mixed—often unknowingly—into street drugs, including heroin, cocaine, and counterfeit pills. This practice allows traffickers to increase the potency of their products with smaller amounts, maximizing their profit margins while significantly increasing overdose risk for users. Fentanyl-laced drugs now account for a staggering proportion of drug overdose deaths, making it one of the most dangerous substances on the market. The drug's lethality is amplified by the fact that it requires only a tiny amount to cause a fatal overdose, meaning users often have no warning before it's too late.

Heroin, methamphetamine, cocaine, and prescription opioids are some of the most commonly abused drugs in the United States. Each of these drugs carries its own unique dangers, and they are responsible for much of the addiction and crime in communities across the country. Heroin, once associated primarily with urban areas, has spread to rural and suburban communities, often serving as a cheaper alternative for those addicted to prescription painkillers. Methamphetamine, known for its intense and prolonged stimulant effects, has seen a resurgence in recent years, largely due to improved manufacturing methods that make it cheaper and more potent. Cocaine remains a popular drug, especially among young adults, and while it lacks the lethality of fentanyl or heroin, it still contributes significantly to addiction and health issues. Prescription opioids, once seen as a safe and legitimate solution for pain management, have proven to be a gateway to addiction for millions, with many users ultimately turning to street drugs when their prescriptions run out or become too expensive.

The overdose crisis has reached record levels, with tens of thousands of Americans losing their lives to drug overdoses each year. Synthetic opioids, primarily fentanyl, are now the leading cause of overdose deaths, a stark shift from previous years when heroin and prescription opioids were more common causes. Families and communities are left reeling from the impact, as overdose deaths often leave behind children, spouses, and parents who must cope with the emotional and financial fallout. In response, communities have scrambled to equip themselves with life-saving tools like naloxone (Narcan), which can reverse opioid overdoses if administered in time. Despite these efforts, the crisis continues to worsen, with overdose rates rising year after year.

Drug-related crime is a pervasive and often overlooked aspect of the crisis. Addiction can drive individuals to engage in various criminal behaviors to support their drug habits, from theft and fraud to violent crimes like assault and robbery. These offenses place a heavy burden on law enforcement agencies and the judicial system, often leading to overcrowded prisons and backlogged courts. In many cases, the cycle of addiction and incarceration becomes a self-perpetuating loop, with individuals struggling to reintegrate into society upon release due to the stigma and lack of support for people with criminal records. The connection between addiction and criminal behavior also extends to the trafficking and distribution networks that operate within communities, bringing with them violence, corruption, and instability.

The social cost of drug addiction extends far beyond the immediate effects on users and their families. Communities bear a substantial burden, as addiction drains resources from schools, public services, and healthcare facilities. Children who grow up in households affected by addiction often suffer emotionally and academically, leading to long-term impacts on their development and future opportunities. The stigma surrounding addiction can also create barriers to treatment, making it more difficult for individuals and families to seek help without fear of judgment or discrimination. Some communities experience a breakdown in social cohesion, as trust erodes and residents become increasingly isolated from one another, leading to a cycle of despair and disconnection that feeds into the addiction problem.

Treatment and recovery options for addiction are often difficult to access, particularly for individuals without insurance or financial means. While many treatment facilities offer detox programs, inpatient rehabilitation, and counseling, the availability of these services varies widely depending on location, income level, and the type of substance being abused. Medication-assisted treatment (MAT) has proven effective for opioid addiction, but it remains underutilized due to stigma, regulatory restrictions, and a lack of awareness among both providers and patients. Barriers to treatment contribute to the cycle of addiction, as individuals are often left to fend for themselves or rely on inadequate resources that fail to address the underlying causes of their addiction.

Government and public health responses to the drug crisis have evolved over time, yet they have struggled to keep pace with the rapidly changing landscape of addiction. Initial efforts focused on criminalizing drug use, leading to decades of punitive policies that disproportionately impacted marginalized communities and did little to curb addiction rates. In recent years, a shift toward harm reduction has gained traction, with programs like needle exchanges, supervised consumption sites, and expanded access to Narcan providing new tools to reduce the immediate harm of drug use. These approaches, while controversial, reflect a growing recognition that addiction is a public health issue rather than merely a criminal problem.

While these efforts are critical, the crisis continues to demand more comprehensive solutions that address the root causes of addiction, crime, and social decay.

The historical evolution of drug use in the United States reflects shifting cultural, social, and economic trends that have shaped society's relationship with substances. Early in U.S. history, drugs like opium and cocaine were widely used and even marketed for their medicinal properties. In the 19th century, opium and cocaine-based tonics were commonplace, with few restrictions on their distribution. As addiction rates rose, public perception began to change, and the early seeds of prohibitionist attitudes took root. By the early 20th century, substances like cocaine, morphine, and heroin had become controlled under the Harrison Narcotics Tax Act of 1914, marking the start of federal drug regulation in the U.S.

The social impacts of drug use began to intensify mid-century, particularly with the rise of marijuana and psychedelics during the countercultural movements of the 1960s. Drug use became intertwined with youth rebellion and anti-establishment sentiment, sparking social backlash and driving government efforts to criminalize a growing number of substances. President Nixon's declaration of a "War on Drugs" in 1971 marked a shift from regulation to aggressive criminalization, setting the tone for decades of drug policy focused on punishment rather than rehabilitation. This "War on Drugs" disproportionately affected low-income and minority communities, with harsh penalties for minor drug offenses leading to the mass incarceration crisis that continues to affect these communities today.

Economic impacts of drug use and addiction ripple across society. At an individual level, addiction can lead to job loss, financial ruin, and long-term poverty, particularly in communities where drug abuse is prevalent. Families often bear the burden of these economic losses, either by supporting addicted loved ones or through the loss of income when addiction disrupts careers and depletes savings. The broader economic impact is staggering; addiction-related healthcare costs, lost productivity, and criminal justice expenses cost the U.S. economy hundreds of billions of dollars each year. This economic toll not only affects individuals but also drains resources from public services, impacting education, infrastructure, and community programs.

Health consequences of drug use are equally severe and multifaceted. Long-term addiction to substances such as heroin, methamphetamine, and opioids has led to rising rates of infectious diseases, including HIV and hepatitis C, due to practices like needle sharing. Chronic drug use also leads to an array of physical and mental health issues, including liver disease, respiratory problems, heart conditions, and severe mental health disorders. Over time, untreated addiction degrades quality of life and reduces life expectancy, creating a public health crisis that further strains the medical system. Mental health issues are common among those struggling with addiction, as substance abuse often co-occurs with conditions like depression, anxiety, and post-traumatic stress disorder (PTSD).

The intertwining of drug use with social, economic, and health issues has produced complex challenges for policymakers, healthcare providers, and community organizations. As addiction has spread across social and economic divides, public attitudes have shifted from seeing it as a personal failing to recognizing it as a disease. This evolving understanding has led to some policy shifts, with recent years seeing a slow movement toward harm reduction and treatment-focused approaches. However, these changes remain limited, as punitive policies from the past continue to shape the landscape of drug enforcement and treatment access, leaving many people trapped in cycles of addiction, poverty, and criminalization.

Each stage of America's evolving relationship with drugs has left its mark on society, from the economic losses and health impacts to the deep-rooted social issues that emerge when entire communities become caught in the cycle of addiction. The ongoing crisis reflects both past policy failures and the continued struggle to balance enforcement with treatment, prevention, and public health efforts. In examining the historical context of drug use and its extensive impacts, the roots of the current epidemic become clearer, underscoring the need for a more comprehensive approach to address this multifaceted problem.

The scope of this book is to provide a comprehensive, multidimensional view of the drug crisis in the United States. It aims to examine the problem from all angles, from the origins of drug production and the international forces driving the supply to the individual and community impacts of addiction and overdose. This includes exploring the role of Mexican and South American cartels, the rise of synthetic drugs like fentanyl, and the social and economic costs of widespread addiction. It also sheds light on how the crisis permeates the criminal justice system, straining resources and entangling individuals in cycles of crime and punishment.

The purpose of this book is to highlight both the severity and complexity of the drug epidemic in America and the urgent need for a multifaceted response. This isn't just a story of addiction; it's a story of international trade, economics, healthcare, crime, and the human spirit. By understanding how these elements intertwine, readers can see why simple solutions fall short and why tackling the drug crisis requires collaboration across multiple sectors. This book aims to break down stigma, educate readers, and offer insights into paths forward, including policy reform, community support, and recovery-focused interventions. For individuals, families, and communities grappling with the effects of addiction, it aims to provide a sense of validation and hope, with a focus on real-world solutions and the resilience within those touched by the crisis.

The Roots of the Crisis

Drug use in the United States has deep historical roots, beginning with the use of opium in the 19th century. Imported primarily from Asia, opium became a popular ingredient in many over-the-counter medicines, often marketed for pain relief or to treat ailments like coughs and stomach issues. Morphine, a derivative of opium, was commonly used as a pain reliever during the Civil War, leading to addiction among soldiers. Cocaine, derived from the coca plant, was also widely used and even endorsed by prominent figures like Sigmund Freud and Thomas Edison, before its addictive properties became widely recognized. These substances were unregulated, easily accessible, and widely accepted for medical and recreational use.

The early 20th century marked the beginning of America's first wave of drug regulations. Concerns over addiction and social issues related to drug use led to the passage of the Pure Food and Drug Act in 1906, which required accurate labeling of medicines and prohibited false claims. The Harrison Narcotics Tax Act of 1914 was a significant turning point, establishing federal regulation over opium and cocaine and imposing taxes on the sale and distribution of these drugs. Though intended to control access to addictive substances, the act effectively criminalized drug possession and use for non-medical purposes, beginning a trend of punitive measures against drug users.

The 1930s saw increased focus on marijuana, with campaigns fueled by racial and social tensions. The Marihuana Tax Act of 1937 imposed heavy taxes on the sale of cannabis, framing it as a dangerous substance tied to violent behavior and targeting Mexican and Black communities who were associated with its use. Anti-drug propaganda of the time, like the infamous film Reefer Madness, portrayed marijuana as a corrupting force, reinforcing negative stereotypes and amplifying public fears. These early policies established the criminalization framework that would later expand to include many other substances.

The post-World War II era brought new drug trends and regulations, especially as synthetic drugs like amphetamines gained popularity. Originally developed as treatment for narcolepsy and depression, amphetamines were widely prescribed and used recreationally by the 1950s. During the same period, psychedelic drugs like LSD entered mainstream awareness, used by some psychiatrists in therapeutic settings and embraced by countercultural movements. In 1970, Congress passed the Controlled Substances Act, creating a federal classification system for drugs based on their medical use and potential for abuse. This act established Schedule I through Schedule V classifications, with Schedule I drugs deemed the most dangerous and lacking medical value. Marijuana, LSD, and heroin were placed in Schedule I, setting the stage for harsher penalties and intensified enforcement.

In 1971, President Richard Nixon officially declared a "War on Drugs," framing drug use as a national threat that required military-style intervention. Federal funding surged for law enforcement, anti-drug campaigns, and international efforts to curb drug trafficking. The creation of the Drug Enforcement Administration (DEA) in 1973 gave the federal government a centralized body dedicated to enforcing drug laws, dramatically increasing arrests and convictions for drug-related offenses. While Nixon's policies initially focused on treatment and prevention, the emphasis quickly shifted toward criminalization, leading to a steep rise in incarceration rates, particularly among minorities and low-income individuals.

The 1980s saw an escalation in anti-drug efforts, spurred by the crack cocaine epidemic. Crack, a cheaper and more addictive form of cocaine, swept through urban areas, leading to a surge in violent crime and drug-related arrests. The Anti-Drug Abuse Act of 1986 introduced mandatory minimum sentences for drug offenses, disproportionately targeting crack cocaine with harsher penalties than powder cocaine. This disparity primarily affected Black communities, with devastating social and economic impacts. First Lady Nancy Reagan's "Just Say No" campaign became synonymous with the decade's zero-tolerance approach, reinforcing the notion that addiction was a matter of personal choice and moral failure rather than a public health issue.

By the 1990s, the impacts of decades of punitive drug policies became apparent. Overcrowded prisons, the devastation of minority communities, and the persistence of drug addiction revealed the limitations of the War on Drugs. At the same time, the emergence of new drugs, including methamphetamine and the beginning of widespread opioid prescriptions, signaled a shift in the types of drugs fueling addiction. The crack epidemic began to fade, but the seeds of a new crisis were sown as pharmaceutical companies aggressively marketed prescription opioids like OxyContin, claiming they posed a low risk of addiction. As opioid prescriptions surged, so did addiction rates, leading to widespread misuse and the eventual rise of heroin as an alternative for those unable to obtain prescriptions.

The early 2000s marked the beginning of a gradual shift in public attitudes toward drug policy. The failures of the War on Drugs, along with the rising opioid crisis, prompted calls for reform and alternative approaches. States began to decriminalize and legalize marijuana, with California leading the way in 1996 by legalizing it for medical use. Public support for drug decriminalization grew as the opioid crisis highlighted the need for treatment and harm reduction rather than punishment. Cities and states started adopting harm reduction strategies, such as needle exchange programs, to combat the spread of infectious diseases among people who inject drugs. The growing awareness of addiction as a chronic, relapsing disease challenged the longstanding view of drug use as solely a criminal issue.

Recent years have seen a continued push toward reform. States across the country have legalized or decriminalized marijuana, and initiatives such as safe injection sites and expanded access to naloxone reflect a more compassionate approach to addiction. The federal government has begun to support treatment and prevention efforts, although punitive policies still persist in many areas. The opioid epidemic has driven lawmakers to prioritize addiction treatment and explore innovative solutions to combat overdose deaths, recognizing that the crisis extends beyond law enforcement's reach.

The history of drug use and policies in the United States reflects a series of evolving attitudes, from early acceptance to criminalization and punishment, to an emerging focus on treatment and prevention. America's approach to drugs has shaped social and economic realities, leaving lasting impacts that continue to influence the nation's response to addiction today. Drug trafficking has woven itself into the American story as an underground economy that bridges global suppliers and domestic demand. The United States, as one of the world's largest consumers of illicit drugs, has become a prime market for traffickers seeking profit and influence. The relationship between American drug demand and international trafficking networks has created a symbiotic system in which drugs, money, and violence continuously flow across borders. Understanding how drug trafficking became a part of America's socio-political landscape reveals a story not only of supply and demand but of systemic failures, global economics, and the evolving tactics of organized crime.

The roots of America's modern drug trafficking networks lie in the political and economic developments of the mid-20th century. After World War II, globalization facilitated a rise in international trade, opening avenues for illegal trafficking alongside legal commerce.

South American and Mexican drug cartels capitalized on these trade routes, moving marijuana, cocaine, and heroin into the United States. By the 1970s and 1980s, the demand for cocaine skyrocketed among affluent Americans, creating unprecedented profits for traffickers and empowering cartels in Colombia and Mexico. Colombian drug lords like Pablo Escobar and the Medellín Cartel rose to power, exerting control over entire regions and establishing violent networks to protect their lucrative trade. The violence associated with these cartels reached American soil as Colombian and Mexican cartels collaborated to supply cocaine and later heroin to the U.S., fueling an era of brutal confrontations between law enforcement and traffickers.

By the 1980s, the crack cocaine epidemic escalated the scale and intensity of drug trafficking. The introduction of crack, a cheaper and smokable form of cocaine, drastically increased the drug's accessibility and popularity in low-income urban areas across the United States. Crack's popularity turned the drug trade into a community-wide problem, leading to violent conflicts among local dealers and gangs who controlled the distribution. Major cities became flashpoints for drug-related crime, leading to increased federal law enforcement intervention. Efforts to combat the crisis, however, largely targeted users and low-level dealers, missing the root of the trafficking networks and exacerbating social and racial tensions.

American intervention in Latin America intensified during this period, as policymakers recognized that the root of drug trafficking was international. The U.S. government launched anti-drug operations in South America, including the infamous "Plan Colombia," which aimed to eradicate coca crops through aerial fumigation, military intervention, and economic incentives. Despite these efforts, coca production continued to thrive as traffickers adapted, often moving production into more remote regions or bribing local officials to look the other way. The economic appeal of coca farming, often the most profitable crop available to impoverished farmers, outweighed the risks, ensuring a steady supply for traffickers. This militarized approach to curbing drug production created significant collateral damage, displacing rural communities and contributing to political instability, while failing to disrupt the cartels' influence.

By the early 2000s, Mexican cartels had risen to dominate drug trafficking into the United States, replacing Colombian cartels as the primary suppliers. The Sinaloa Cartel, led by Joaquin "El Chapo" Guzmán, became one of the most powerful criminal organizations in the world, controlling vast portions of the drug trade across North and Central America. The cartel's tactics were ruthless, using violence and corruption to expand its territory and eliminate competitors. Mexican cartels diversified their drug portfolio, adding heroin and methamphetamine to their operations and further embedding themselves in American markets. Heroin's popularity soared as opioid addiction surged across the U.S., creating new demand that Mexican traffickers quickly supplied. Methamphetamine production and trafficking, once dominated by small, domestic "meth labs," shifted to large-scale operations run by Mexican cartels, which could produce the drug more cheaply and efficiently.

The spread of fentanyl, a synthetic opioid up to 100 times more potent than morphine, introduced a new and deadly chapter in drug trafficking. Initially manufactured in pharmaceutical settings, fentanyl entered the black market through both legitimate and illicit supply chains. Mexican cartels recognized fentanyl's profitability, often sourcing raw materials from China and producing counterfeit pills or lacing other drugs with fentanyl to increase potency. These fentanyl-laced drugs found their way into heroin, cocaine, and methamphetamine supplies, dramatically increasing overdose deaths. The opioid crisis—first fueled by overprescription and then sustained by illegal opioids like heroin and fentanyl—deepened the drug trafficking problem, pushing both public health and law enforcement systems to their limits.

The financial underpinnings of drug trafficking reveal its vast economic impact on both sides of the border. Drug trafficking generates billions of dollars annually, with profits laundered through complex networks of shell companies, offshore accounts, and legitimate businesses. Cartels invest their earnings in real estate, luxury goods, and businesses, legitimizing their profits while strengthening their control. In the United States, cash generated from drug sales flows back to cartels through intricate money-laundering operations. Drug trafficking's financial power enables cartels to bribe officials, fund armed militias, and support communities within their territories, establishing a type of narco-economy that intertwines with the legitimate economy in both Mexico and the U.S. As a result, drug trafficking not only perpetuates addiction but also destabilizes economies and institutions, particularly in regions where cartel influence is strongest.

The criminal justice system's response to drug trafficking has been a complex and often controversial aspect of America's approach. Increased militarization of the U.S.-Mexico border, high-profile drug busts, and strict sentencing laws for trafficking-related offenses underscore the law enforcement emphasis on stopping drug flow at its source. However, these efforts often target individual traffickers or low-level participants rather than dismantling the cartels themselves, which continuously adapt to evade detection. Mass incarceration policies have filled U.S. prisons with individuals involved in the drug trade, leading to overcrowded prison systems and the criminalization of addiction. Meanwhile, cartels continue to evolve their methods, using underground tunnels, drones, and sophisticated smuggling techniques to bypass border enforcement. The heavy emphasis on criminal justice solutions has led to unintended consequences, reinforcing cycles of poverty and crime within communities most affected by drug trafficking.

Drug trafficking's influence extends to American communities in ways that go beyond substance abuse, creating an ecosystem of crime, violence, and economic strain. In neighborhoods where drug markets are entrenched, crime rates rise as gangs and local dealers compete for territory. Violence becomes commonplace, with shootings, robberies, and assaults linked to drug deals and territorial disputes. This cycle of violence affects not only those involved in the drug trade but also residents who live in constant fear of becoming collateral damage. Schools, community organizations, and local businesses struggle to function in environments overshadowed by the drug trade, as resources are diverted to cope with the effects of addiction, poverty, and violence. Drug trafficking shapes these communities at a fundamental level, perpetuating generational cycles of hardship and criminalization.

The impact of drug trafficking on American society has also shaped public attitudes toward drug policy and law enforcement. As addiction and overdose rates rise, many Americans question the effectiveness of punitive measures, calling for a shift from criminalization to treatment-focused approaches. Cities and states have begun to implement harm reduction strategies, such as syringe exchange programs and safe consumption sites, to mitigate the immediate risks of drug use. Policymakers have explored ways to cut off drug trafficking at its source, including economic and diplomatic efforts to reduce production in supply countries. However, the sheer scale of the drug trade and the deeply embedded economic incentives make dismantling these networks a formidable task. Drug trafficking's resilience underscores the need for a comprehensive response that addresses both supply and demand, moving beyond law enforcement to include healthcare, social services, and economic reform.

The globalization of drug trafficking has intertwined it with larger geopolitical dynamics, shaping U.S. foreign policy and international relations. Relations with Mexico, in particular, have been shaped by shared challenges in combating cartels and securing the border. Joint efforts like the Mérida Initiative, which provided funding and resources to combat organized crime in Mexico, highlight the collaborative nature of modern anti-drug efforts. However, political tensions over immigration, border security, and violence complicate these partnerships. At the same time, U.S. demand for drugs perpetuates the need for these foreign alliances, creating a cycle in which America's appetite for narcotics sustains the very criminal organizations that the government seeks to dismantle. This cycle of dependency fuels the broader story of drug trafficking, tying America's domestic crisis to international dynamics that impact diplomacy, trade, and regional stability.

American cities have become epicenters for the distribution and sale of illicit drugs, with major hubs like Los Angeles, New York, Chicago, and Miami serving as key nodes in trafficking networks. Each city presents unique logistical advantages, from coastal access to extensive transportation infrastructure, allowing traffickers to move products across the country quickly. Urban centers, where large populations create high demand, are particularly vulnerable to trafficking-related violence and crime. Smaller cities and rural areas have also seen an increase in drug trafficking activity, often as cartels target regions where law enforcement is less equipped to combat organized crime. This widespread penetration of the drug trade has made trafficking a part of everyday American life, reaching from bustling metropolises to quiet rural towns.

The continuous evolution of drug trafficking tactics and the adaptive nature of cartels underscore the challenge of effectively combating the drug trade. As law enforcement disrupts one trafficking route, cartels find new methods and locations to continue their operations. Tunnels beneath the U.S.-Mexico border, for instance, have become increasingly elaborate, equipped with lighting, ventilation, and even rail systems to move products efficiently. Cartels also exploit technology, using encrypted messaging, GPS tracking, and drones to coordinate shipments and evade detection. These innovations enable traffickers to maintain a steady supply of drugs to the U.S., showcasing the resilience and resourcefulness of criminal organizations that thrive on America's persistent demand for narcotics.

Drug trafficking has firmly embedded itself in the American story, shaping not only individual lives but also national policies, Drug trafficking has firmly embedded itself in the American story, shaping not only individual lives but also national policies, economic structures, and social realities. Its influence is pervasive, as it fuels a cycle of violence, addiction, and crime that transcends borders and communities, affecting every level of society. The powerful, profitable, and adaptive nature of trafficking networks makes it a complex issue that defies simple solutions, evolving faster than policy changes or enforcement measures can keep up.

The supply chain of the drug trade—spanning cultivation, production, distribution, and sale—is a sophisticated operation rooted in a web of political and economic realities. Cartels operate as corporations, with hierarchies, territories, and specialized roles, from the cultivators in the Andes mountains to the chemists in clandestine labs, to the distributors in American cities. In Mexico, Guatemala, and Colombia, rural communities often rely on coca and poppy cultivation as economic lifelines, as legal crops cannot provide comparable income. In these regions, cartel-controlled economies sometimes offer protection and support to locals, fostering loyalty and complicity that can shield traffickers from law enforcement. The socioeconomic conditions that sustain this workforce highlight the global dimensions of America's drug crisis, where poverty and limited opportunities in producer countries drive participation in the illicit drug trade.

Drug trafficking has not only fueled the rise of organized crime but also bred an entire infrastructure of corruption and violence across the Americas. In Mexico, cartels have become powerful political entities, bribing local police, judges, and government officials to protect their interests and eliminate threats. Politicians and law enforcement agents are often coerced or incentivized into working with cartels, leading to deep-rooted corruption that compromises anti-drug efforts. Many police officers in Mexico and other drug-producing countries face dangerous pressure, as refusing a cartel's offer can mean threats to their lives or their families. Entire towns have been terrorized by the presence of cartels, whose violent enforcement tactics often spill over into civilian life, resulting in massacres, public executions, and disappearances that destabilize entire communities.

The United States, while less visibly affected by cartel violence, faces its own challenges in law enforcement corruption linked to drug trafficking. The significant profits involved create a temptation for individuals within various sectors to participate in trafficking-related activities, whether by aiding smuggling operations or accepting bribes in exchange for ignoring shipments. The sheer volume of drugs crossing the U.S.-Mexico border has overwhelmed border enforcement efforts, and although agents continually adapt, traffickers remain one step ahead, with sophisticated concealment methods, tunnels, and bribery schemes. This infiltration into law enforcement underscores the difficulty of eradicating drug trafficking at the supply level and highlights the far-reaching influence of the drug economy.

The rise of synthetic drugs has further complicated the trafficking landscape, as synthetic opioids, stimulants, and novel psychoactive substances (NPS) continue to diversify the illicit drug market. Unlike plant-based drugs like cocaine or heroin, synthetic drugs like fentanyl and methamphetamine can be manufactured in large quantities with minimal infrastructure. Fentanyl production in particular has surged, as small amounts of the drug produce powerful effects, making it ideal for traffickers seeking maximum profitability with minimal material investment. The potent and profitable nature of synthetic drugs has made them a focus for traffickers, who can produce them domestically or import key chemicals from countries like China. This shift from natural to synthetic drugs has exacerbated the overdose crisis in the U.S., as drugs laced with fentanyl often result in fatal consequences for users unaware of its presence.

The advent of digital communication and online marketplaces has further transformed drug trafficking, as traffickers and buyers now leverage the anonymity of the internet. The "dark web," a network of hidden websites accessed through special browsers, has become a popular venue for drug transactions, where users can purchase everything from cannabis to fentanyl with a few clicks. Cryptocurrencies like Bitcoin facilitate these transactions, providing a level of privacy that complicates law enforcement efforts to trace and prosecute. Online marketplaces give both traffickers and users unprecedented access to a wide range of substances, bypassing the need for street-level dealers and increasing the accessibility of drugs to new audiences. Although law enforcement agencies have shut down some prominent dark web marketplaces, others quickly emerge, underscoring the adaptability of traffickers and the difficulty of curbing online drug sales.

Drug trafficking also intersects with human trafficking, arms trafficking, and other illegal activities, compounding its impact on communities and law enforcement. Cartels often diversify their operations, moving beyond drug sales to smuggling weapons and people across borders, creating a complex network of interrelated crimes. These crossovers provide cartels with diversified revenue streams and increase their ability to control and influence multiple areas of criminal enterprise. The proliferation of arms trafficking in particular has increased the level of violence in drug-producing and drug-trafficking regions, as cartels obtain military-grade weapons to assert dominance over competitors and resist law enforcement. The interconnected nature of these crimes has profound social consequences, as trafficking networks fuel cycles of violence, displacement, and fear.

In urban and rural communities across the United States, the presence of drug trafficking has reshaped social dynamics and exacerbated economic disparities. In cities, traffickers rely on gangs and local organizations to distribute drugs, leading to territorial disputes and violent confrontations. As a result, neighborhoods with high rates of drug trafficking often experience increased violence, deteriorating social cohesion, and decreased quality of life for residents. In rural areas, methamphetamine and opioid trafficking have similarly devastating effects, straining already limited resources for healthcare, education, and social services. Law enforcement in these areas faces unique challenges, as they may lack the manpower and resources to combat large-scale trafficking operations, leaving communities vulnerable to the drug trade's influence.

The impact of drug trafficking on American families and public health is undeniable, as addiction tears through communities, leaving trauma and loss in its wake. Families facing the fallout of addiction often endure cycles of crisis, from financial strain to loss of employment, housing, and social stability. Children of individuals involved in trafficking or substance use are at high risk of neglect, abuse, and emotional hardship, which can perpetuate cycles of addiction and crime within families. Public health systems, already stretched thin, struggle to address the wave of drug-related health issues, from overdoses to infectious diseases spread through needle sharing. Treatment facilities, mental health services, and social support networks are often ill-equipped to handle the scale of need, and many communities lack adequate resources to support those seeking recovery.

The economic toll of drug trafficking on the United States extends to costs associated with law enforcement, healthcare, lost productivity, and social services. Incarceration, court proceedings, drug treatment programs, emergency medical care, and other interventions carry significant financial burdens. According to estimates, the total cost of drug-related issues in the U.S. reaches hundreds of billions of dollars annually. Employers also bear the weight of drug-related absenteeism, decreased productivity, and workplace accidents, which affect overall economic output. Communities that face high rates of addiction often experience reduced property values, deterred investment, and diminished economic opportunities. The long-term costs of the drug trade are vast, affecting both public institutions and private industry, highlighting the need for sustainable solutions that address the root causes of drug demand and trafficking.

Drug trafficking's influence on American culture has also left an indelible mark on popular media, fashion, and music. Stories of cartel leaders, narco-culture, and the gritty realities of the drug trade have become fixtures in film, television, and literature. Shows like Narcos and films like Scarface dramatize the lives of traffickers and the violence of the drug world, glamorizing and sensationalizing aspects of trafficking. Rap and hip-hop music, in particular, often reference drug culture, both as a means of critiquing social realities and as a reflection of the lived experiences of communities impacted by trafficking. The cultural normalization of drug trafficking and its association with wealth and power contribute to a complex relationship between society and the drug trade, where fascination coexists with condemnation.

Attempts to combat drug trafficking have increasingly moved toward harm reduction and treatment-based approaches, as policymakers recognize the limitations of punitive measures. Some cities have implemented initiatives like supervised injection sites, needle exchange programs, and expanded access to naloxone, an opioid overdose antidote, to reduce the immediate risks associated with drug use. These programs acknowledge the realities of drug trafficking's influence on public health, aiming to save lives and support recovery rather than punish addiction. Lawmakers are also exploring broader drug policy reforms, including decriminalization and legalization measures, to decrease the power of traffickers by reducing the illicit drug market. While these approaches remain controversial, they represent a shift toward addressing the systemic causes and effects of drug trafficking rather than solely focusing on enforcement.

Despite decades of efforts to dismantle trafficking networks, drug trafficking's adaptability and resilience have made it a permanent fixture in American society. As trafficking networks become more sophisticated, policymakers and law enforcement must continuously innovate to keep up. Addressing the drug crisis requires a nuanced approach that goes beyond border enforcement and criminal justice, recognizing that drug trafficking is deeply rooted in social, economic, and health issues. Solutions must encompass treatment, education, harm reduction, and international cooperation, focusing on reducing demand while disrupting supply chains. The story of drug trafficking in America is ongoing, as the country grapples with finding sustainable responses to a complex crisis that has reshaped its communities, institutions, and way of life.

Early efforts to curb drug use in the United States reflect a century-long attempt to control and mitigate the effects of drug consumption through regulation, criminalization, and treatment initiatives. From the first restrictive laws in the early 1900s to the aggressive war on drugs in the late 20th century, the United States has continuously sought ways to manage drug use. Each wave of anti-drug efforts has left a unique mark on American society, shaping attitudes, policies, and the criminal justice landscape. These early policies offer valuable insight into how the nation's approach to drug control evolved and the societal and cultural forces that influenced this evolution.

The United States first formally regulated drugs in the early 20th century, beginning with the Pure Food and Drug Act of 1906. This legislation marked the government's initial step into regulating consumer goods, including drugs. The act required accurate labeling of medications and aimed to eliminate dangerous adulterants in food and drugs, thereby indirectly addressing issues of drug misuse and overconsumption. Before this, opiates, cocaine, and other substances were freely available in over-the-counter products, used as tonics, and sold as remedies for various ailments. Popular products like "Mrs. Winslow's Soothing Syrup," which contained morphine, were widely used, particularly among middle- and upper-class Americans. The Pure Food and Drug Act reflected growing public concern over the unregulated drug market, though it targeted misleading advertising and unregulated manufacturing rather than drug use itself.

However, the 1914 Harrison Narcotics Tax Act marked a significant shift from consumer protection to direct regulation of drug distribution. The law required manufacturers, importers, and physicians to register and pay taxes on opium, morphine, and cocaine products, aiming to control access to these drugs by restricting their distribution. Although framed as a tax law, the Harrison Act placed a substantial burden on medical professionals and soon restricted physicians' ability to prescribe narcotics to addicts. This created a divide between the medical community and law enforcement, as doctors and pharmacists who continued to provide opiates to those with addiction risked arrest and prosecution. The act inadvertently criminalized addiction by limiting legal access to drugs, pushing many individuals toward illicit sources and marking the beginning of the criminalization of drug users in America.

The effects of the Harrison Act laid the groundwork for future anti-drug policies by establishing a precedent of government intervention and regulation. Following the act's passage, law enforcement became more involved in drug regulation, setting the stage for a punitive approach to drug control. Individuals who had previously relied on medical prescriptions found themselves labeled as criminals, leading to the creation of a black market for opiates. This criminalization of drug use brought with it a wave of social stigmatization, as addiction became increasingly associated with criminality rather than viewed as a medical or psychological issue. The act also laid the foundation for future laws by treating drug use as a legal problem to be managed through enforcement rather than a health issue to be addressed through treatment.

As drug use continued to evolve, so too did the approach to controlling it. In the 1930s, the Federal Bureau of Narcotics (FBN) emerged under the leadership of Commissioner Harry J. Anslinger, who would become one of the most influential figures in American drug policy. Anslinger led aggressive anti-drug campaigns that associated drugs, particularly marijuana, with crime and moral decay. During his tenure, the FBN propagated sensationalized narratives linking marijuana use to violence, criminality, and racial minorities, fueling public fear and reinforcing negative stereotypes. Anslinger's campaign culminated in the passage of the Marihuana Tax Act of 1937, which effectively outlawed cannabis by placing strict regulations and prohibitive taxes on its sale and cultivation. The act criminalized marijuana at a federal level, setting a precedent for how future policies would categorize and handle drug control.

Anslinger's campaign against marijuana also marked the beginning of racialized drug enforcement in the United States. The FBN's rhetoric often associated cannabis use with Mexican immigrants and Black communities, exploiting racial prejudices to justify strict regulation. This racialized approach laid the groundwork for later policies that disproportionately impacted marginalized communities, leading to systemic disparities in drug-related arrests and sentencing. The anti-marijuana campaign reflected broader social tensions and racial anxieties of the time, as drug policy became a tool for controlling specific populations under the guise of public safety. The legacy of these policies persists today, as racial bias in drug enforcement remains a critical issue within the American criminal justice system.

In response to growing concerns about drug use in the 1960s and 1970s, the U.S. government began to adopt a more organized approach to drug control. The Controlled Substances Act (CSA) of 1970 was a landmark piece of legislation that classified drugs into five "schedules" based on their medical use and potential for abuse. Under the CSA, drugs with high potential for abuse and no accepted medical use, like heroin and LSD, were placed in Schedule I, while drugs with medical applications, such as amphetamines, were classified in lower schedules. The CSA provided a framework for federal drug enforcement and marked the beginning of a coordinated federal effort to regulate drug use. The act also introduced significant federal involvement in the categorization of substances, placing many psychoactive drugs under federal control, even if states had differing perspectives on drug classification and enforcement.

However, the CSA's scheduling system has faced criticism for its rigid classifications, particularly regarding marijuana, which remains a Schedule I substance despite growing evidence of its medical

The Cartel Connection

The fight against drug trafficking in the United States is a battle marked by complexity and relentless competition, where powerful cartels operate with near-military precision. Over decades, these organizations have evolved, adapting their strategies to outmaneuver law enforcement and exploit vulnerabilities in the market. Their influence extends far beyond the borders of Mexico, infiltrating American communities and driving a cycle of violence, addiction, and economic devastation. As the drug crisis continues to escalate, understanding the major cartels behind this epidemic is crucial in grasping the depth of the challenge faced by authorities and communities alike.

The Sinaloa Cartel, often referred to as the "crown jewel" of drug trafficking organizations in Mexico, stands as a testament to the complex interplay of power, violence, and illicit trade. Founded in the late 1980s, this cartel emerged from the mountainous region of Sinaloa, transforming from a modest coalition of local growers and traffickers into a colossal criminal enterprise that has significantly shaped the landscape of drug trafficking in North America. Its operations have extended far beyond the borders of Mexico, establishing a vast and intricate distribution network that penetrates major U.S. cities, fueling addiction and violence across communities.

At the helm of this organization was Joaquín "El Chapo" Guzmán, a figure whose life reads like a gripping novel filled with daring escapes and ruthless ambition. Guzmán's rise to power was marked by a combination of calculated brutality and a keen understanding of the importance of community relations. He not only forged alliances with corrupt officials and local law enforcement but also strategically endeared himself to the communities from which his operations thrived. This duality allowed the Sinaloa Cartel to maintain a stronghold over crucial trafficking routes, often evading law enforcement's grip while minimizing competition from rival cartels. The Sinaloa Cartel became infamous for its ability to adapt quickly to challenges, employing sophisticated smuggling tactics that included elaborate tunnel networks stretching beneath the U.S.-Mexico border— a hallmark of their operations that highlighted their ingenuity and determination.

El Chapo's eventual capture and imprisonment in 2016 could have spelled doom for the cartel. However, rather than collapse under the weight of increased scrutiny and law enforcement pressure, the Sinaloa Cartel showcased an extraordinary resilience. Under the leadership of Ismael "El Mayo" Zambada, a seasoned and strategic figure in his own right, the cartel diversified its operations and leadership structure. Zambada's approach emphasized a continued commitment to maintaining influence and control while navigating the increasingly volatile drug market. This adaptability has allowed the Sinaloa Cartel to remain a dominant player in the industry, even as rivals emerge and law enforcement strategies evolve.

In recent years, the cartel has shifted its focus to the production of synthetic drugs, particularly fentanyl, a potent opioid that has become a central player in America's escalating overdose crisis. Fentanyl, often mixed with other drugs like heroin and cocaine, has dramatically increased the risk of overdose among users, leading to devastating consequences across the nation. The Sinaloa Cartel has skillfully established connections with Chinese suppliers of precursor chemicals, enabling it to manufacture fentanyl and its analogs on a massive scale. This strategic pivot not only underscores the cartel's ability to adapt to market demands but also reflects a chilling awareness of the lethal potential of its products.

The emergence of fentanyl as a significant component of the cartel's operations has irrevocably altered the landscape of the drug trade. It serves as a stark reminder of the escalating sophistication and brutality of drug trafficking organizations. The Sinaloa Cartel's capacity to innovate in response to law enforcement efforts and shifting drug trends is a chilling reflection of its determination to maintain its grip on the market. With each passing year, the cartel's influence continues to expand, leaving a path of devastation in its wake, characterized by increased addiction rates, rising crime, and countless lives lost to overdose.

The Sinaloa Cartel's impact extends beyond the immediate consequences of drug trafficking. Its operations have significant socio-economic repercussions, influencing everything from local economies to health care systems in the communities it touches. The violence and instability generated by the cartel's activities ripple through society, perpetuating cycles of poverty, addiction, and crime. As communities grapple with the fallout of addiction and violence, the Sinaloa Cartel remains a formidable force, illustrating the complexities of confronting such entrenched criminal networks.

As we explore the Sinaloa Cartel's intricate web of operations, it becomes clear that this organization is not just a mere player in the drug trade; it is a defining force shaping the realities of countless lives. The cartel's adaptability, strategic foresight, and ruthless ambition paint a portrait of a criminal empire that is as captivating as it is terrifying. The Sinaloa Cartel stands as a stark reminder of the profound challenges that lie ahead in the fight against drug trafficking and its far-reaching implications for society as a whole.

The Jalisco New Generation Cartel (CJNG) has rapidly ascended to prominence in the pantheon of Mexico's drug trafficking organizations, establishing itself as one of the most formidable and feared cartels in the world. Emerging from the ashes of the Milenio Cartel in the early 2010s, the CJNG has distinguished itself not just by the scale of its operations, but also through its willingness to employ extreme violence and ruthlessness. Under the leadership of Nemesio Oseguera Cervantes, infamously known as "El Mencho," the cartel has expanded its reach beyond traditional drug trafficking into a wide array of criminal enterprises, including extortion, kidnapping, and human trafficking. This diversification has fortified its position in the criminal underworld, allowing it to adapt and thrive amidst fierce competition and constant law enforcement scrutiny.

The CJNG's operations span vast regions across Mexico, where it has established a strong foothold in key trafficking corridors. Its influence has quickly permeated the United States, where it competes head-to-head with established cartels, most notably the Sinaloa Cartel, for control of lucrative drug markets. Unlike its rivals, the CJNG's approach to territorial control is characterized by rapid, brutal enforcement. The cartel engages in violent clashes with rival gangs, often resulting in bloodshed that spills into public spaces. This aggressive posture serves a dual purpose: it asserts dominance over contested territories while instilling a pervasive sense of fear among both competitors and the general population.

The CJNG's distribution network is extensive and efficient, enabling it to supply a wide variety of drugs, including methamphetamine, cocaine, and heroin. However, it has placed particular emphasis on the production and trafficking of fentanyl, a potent synthetic opioid that has contributed significantly to the ongoing opioid crisis in the United States. The cartel's ability to manufacture fentanyl and its analogs underscores its adaptability and resourcefulness, as it responds to shifting market demands and the escalating appetite for more lethal substances.

The cartel's meteoric rise has not come without consequences, particularly regarding violence in Mexico. The CJNG is infamous for its brutal tactics, which include public displays of violence, mass killings, and high-profile assassinations aimed at rival cartel leaders. These methods are not only a means of asserting dominance; they are also a strategic choice designed to send a chilling message to both enemies and the public. Such displays of brutality have contributed to a dramatic increase in homicide rates in areas under the cartel's influence, casting a long shadow over communities already grappling with poverty and instability.

The CJNG's actions have drawn the ire of both Mexican and U.S. authorities. Recognizing the cartel as a significant threat, the U.S. government has implemented a series of sanctions and law enforcement initiatives aimed at dismantling its operations. Despite these efforts, the CJNG has proven remarkably resilient, often sidestepping law enforcement's best efforts to curtail its influence. The cartel's ability to adapt quickly to law enforcement pressure—shifting operations, changing leadership, and diversifying its criminal activities—demonstrates a level of sophistication and tenacity that is both alarming and captivating.

El Mencho's leadership style further exemplifies the cartel's relentless pursuit of power. He operates with a blend of calculated strategy and brute force, employing a network of loyal operatives and hitmen to carry out his orders. Under his command, the CJNG has embraced a philosophy of aggression, believing that fear is the most effective tool for maintaining control. This mindset has led to an escalation in violence not only within Mexico but also spilling across the border into the United States, where the cartel vies for dominance in key drug markets.

As the CJNG continues to assert its influence, its impact on communities cannot be overstated. Families torn apart by addiction, neighborhoods plagued by violence, and law enforcement stretched thin by the relentless onslaught of criminal activity paint a grim picture of the reality in regions affected by the cartel's reach. The opioid crisis, fueled in part by the CJNG's production of fentanyl, has left countless lives shattered, forcing communities to grapple with the fallout of addiction, overdose deaths, and crime.

The rise of the Jalisco New Generation Cartel is a compelling saga of ambition, brutality, and resilience. It exemplifies the dark allure of the drug trade, showcasing how power dynamics shift within the criminal underworld. The cartel's meteoric rise, marked by its willingness to employ extreme violence and diversify its operations, has redefined the landscape of drug trafficking in Mexico and beyond. As we delve deeper into the world of the CJNG, it becomes evident that understanding this cartel is crucial to grasping the broader implications of the ongoing drug crisis—one that continues to evolve in both complexity and impact.

The Gulf Cartel stands as one of the oldest and most storied drug trafficking organizations in Mexico, with a history that stretches back to the 1930s. Initially focused on the cultivation and trafficking of marijuana, the cartel evolved throughout the decades, expanding its operations to include cocaine and other illicit substances by the 1980s. Based in the northeastern state of Tamaulipas, the Gulf Cartel occupies a strategically advantageous position along vital smuggling routes leading into the United States. This geographic advantage has been a critical factor in the cartel's ability to thrive, allowing it to exert influence over key trafficking corridors for generations.

Throughout its long history, the Gulf Cartel has engaged in a series of collaborations with various criminal organizations, most notably with the Zetas. Originally formed as the armed wing of the Gulf Cartel, the Zetas eventually broke away to establish their own cartel, igniting a violent conflict that would have lasting ramifications for both organizations. This split marked a significant turning point for the Gulf Cartel, as it found itself embroiled in a brutal power struggle that decimated its ranks and reputation. The violent fallout from this internal strife resulted in significant casualties, leading to a marked decline in the Gulf Cartel's influence in the drug trade.

Despite these challenges, the Gulf Cartel has shown remarkable resilience. The organization has adapted its operations to the changing landscape of drug trafficking, focusing on maintaining control over local routes while developing new methods for smuggling drugs into the United States. While its prominence may have waned in comparison to newer cartels like the Sinaloa and Jalisco New Generation Cartel (CJNG), the Gulf Cartel remains a significant player in the drug trade, continuing to facilitate the smuggling of cocaine, marijuana, and methamphetamine across the border.

The Gulf Cartel's operations are characterized by a combination of established networks and shifting alliances, allowing it to navigate the complexities of the drug trade effectively. While its former dominance has been challenged, the cartel has maintained a presence in key markets, leveraging its experience and historical connections to sustain its operations. The Gulf Cartel's adaptability is evident in its efforts to modernize its strategies, often employing more sophisticated techniques for smuggling and distribution.

The cartel's longstanding history has also fostered a culture of violence and corruption that permeates the regions it controls. Over the years, the Gulf Cartel has been associated with numerous violent incidents, from gruesome public displays to targeted assassinations, aimed at asserting dominance over rival organizations and instilling fear in local communities. This culture of violence has not only contributed to a significant rise in crime rates in areas under its influence but has also prompted a violent response from law enforcement and rival factions.

Despite the challenges posed by rival cartels and law enforcement efforts, the Gulf Cartel has maintained its operational resilience. The cartel has demonstrated an ability to regroup and reorganize after significant setbacks, often relying on established networks and the loyalty of long-time operatives. This tenacity underscores the complexity of the drug trade, where power dynamics can shift rapidly, and survival often hinges on a cartel's ability to adapt to changing circumstances.

In recent years, as the landscape of drug trafficking in Mexico has evolved, the Gulf Cartel has faced new threats from emerging organizations. The Zetas, once its allies, have transformed into fierce competitors, employing their own violent tactics to claim territory and influence. This rivalry has led to intensified violence in regions where the Gulf Cartel operates, as it struggles to maintain its foothold against the encroachment of both the Zetas and newer entrants into the drug trade. The result has been a volatile environment characterized by turf wars, assassinations, and an ongoing battle for control over lucrative drug routes.

The Gulf Cartel's legacy is a complex tapestry woven with threads of ambition, violence, and resilience. Its history reflects the broader narrative of drug trafficking in Mexico, marked by shifting alliances, violent confrontations, and the persistent quest for power. As the cartel continues to navigate the challenges of an evolving drug trade, its impact on local communities, law enforcement, and rival organizations remains significant. The Gulf Cartel's story is far from over; it continues to adapt and endure, leaving an indelible mark on the landscape of drug trafficking in the United States and beyond.

The Beltrán Leyva Organization (BLO) emerged in the early 2000s as a formidable force in the Mexican drug trade, initially operating as a faction within the Sinaloa Cartel. Founded by the Beltrán Leyva brothers, the organization gained traction and influence in the drug trafficking landscape, leveraging its connections and experience gained while allied with the Sinaloa Cartel. However, a seismic shift occurred following the arrest of one of its key leaders, prompting the BLO to sever ties with its former allies. This break marked the beginning of a fierce and violent chapter in the Mexican drug war, as the BLO established itself as an independent entity with its own trafficking routes and distribution networks.

In the wake of its separation from the Sinaloa Cartel, the BLO quickly adapted to the changing dynamics of the drug trade. It developed its own operational strategies, focusing on trafficking cocaine and heroin into the United States. The organization made significant inroads into key markets, particularly in the Northeast, where its presence contributed to the rising tide of addiction and violence. The BLO became notorious for its ruthless enforcement tactics, often resorting to extreme violence to eliminate rivals and intimidate law enforcement. This penchant for brutality not only solidified its reputation within the drug trade but also drew the attention of authorities, intensifying law enforcement efforts to dismantle the organization.

The BLO's rise was characterized by a series of violent confrontations with rival cartels, including the Sinaloa Cartel and the Jalisco New Generation Cartel (CJNG). As the BLO sought to carve out its own territory and assert its dominance, it engaged in brutal turf wars, often resulting in public massacres and gruesome displays of violence. These tactics were designed to send a clear message to both enemies and potential informants, fostering a climate of fear that allowed the BLO to operate with relative impunity in its early years. However, the escalation of violence not only drew law enforcement's ire but also alienated local communities, which began to suffer the consequences of the cartel's brutal methods.

The organization's involvement in various criminal activities extended beyond drug trafficking. Kidnapping and extortion became staples of the BLO's operations, providing additional revenue streams while instilling fear in the populations they preyed upon. This diversification of criminal enterprise showcased the BLO's adaptability in the face of increased pressure from law enforcement and rival factions. The cartel's ability to exploit weaknesses in local governance and community structures allowed it to maintain a foothold in key regions, even as competition intensified.

Despite its initial success, the BLO's fortunes began to wane as internal fragmentation and external pressures took their toll. The organization's leadership faced a series of arrests and killings, leading to a decline in cohesive operations. As key figures were removed from power, factions within the BLO splintered, leading to a loss of control and influence over its established routes. This fragmentation weakened the cartel's ability to maintain its dominance in the drug trade, paving the way for rival organizations to encroach on its territory.

In recent years, remnants of the BLO have continued to operate, albeit at a diminished capacity. These factions often engage in violent skirmishes with rival cartels, perpetuating a cycle of violence and instability in regions still grappling with the aftermath of cartel wars. The ongoing presence of the BLO, despite its decline, serves as a grim reminder of the complexities of the drug trade in Mexico. Local communities remain caught in the crossfire, as the remnants of the BLO and rival cartels vie for control over lucrative trafficking routes.

The legacy of the Beltrán Leyva Organization is a chilling chapter in the saga of Mexico's drug war. Its initial emergence as a powerful entity within the Sinaloa Cartel, followed by a tumultuous breakaway, underscores the volatile nature of cartel dynamics and the brutal reality of drug trafficking. The BLO's history is marked by violence, ambition, and eventual fragmentation, reflecting the broader struggles faced by many cartels in an ever-evolving landscape. As the BLO continues to cast a long shadow over regions in Mexico, the impacts of its actions resonate far beyond the borders, contributing to the ongoing crisis of addiction and violence in the United States.

The La Familia Michoacana cartel, hailing from the state of Michoacán, presents a complex and multifaceted narrative within the broader context of Mexican organized crime. Founded in the early 2000s, the organization initially emerged as a self-defense group. Its primary aim was to combat the pervasive violence inflicted by rival cartels and to protect the local communities that had been caught in the crossfire of escalating drug wars. This grassroots origin story allowed La Familia to position itself as a protector of the people, a narrative that it would later leverage to gain both influence and legitimacy.

From its inception, La Familia Michoacana differentiated itself from other cartels through its unique blend of violence and a quasi-religious ideology. The cartel espoused a moral framework that justified its actions under the guise of community defense, promoting a code of conduct that members were expected to adhere to. This ideology was heavily influenced by a distorted interpretation of Christian principles, which framed their operations as a righteous endeavor against corruption and vice. This narrative was not only a recruiting tool but also a means to foster loyalty among local residents who were disillusioned by the violence of other criminal organizations. La Familia presented itself as a counterbalance to the brutality of rival cartels, seeking to cultivate an image of social responsibility amid its violent undertakings.

As La Familia transitioned from a self-defense group to a full-fledged drug trafficking organization, it rapidly capitalized on the lucrative methamphetamine trade. The cartel became notorious for its production of high-quality meth, establishing extensive networks to distribute this drug throughout Mexico and into the United States. By focusing on methamphetamine, La Familia was able to tap into a growing market that was becoming increasingly dominated by addiction and demand. The cartel's operations were marked by a sophisticated production process, which included not only the cultivation of precursor chemicals but also the establishment of clandestine laboratories capable of producing large quantities of the drug.

The cartel's unique approach to drug trafficking also included a strategy of community involvement, which set it apart from many of its rivals. La Familia often engaged in the provision of social services, including healthcare, education, and economic support, to local residents. This investment in the community was a deliberate tactic designed to build loyalty and foster a sense of obligation among the populace. By presenting itself as a benefactor, La Familia aimed to create a buffer against law enforcement efforts and to insulate itself from public resentment. This strategy proved effective in many areas, as local communities often viewed the cartel as a necessary evil in a landscape marked by violence and instability.

Despite its initial success, La Familia Michoacana faced significant challenges, particularly as rival organizations began to emerge and encroach on its territory. The rise of the Jalisco New Generation Cartel (CJNG) marked a turning point for La Familia, as the CJNG employed aggressive tactics and brutal violence in its quest for dominance. The competition for control over lucrative drug routes and production areas led to intense conflict, resulting in significant casualties on both sides. This internecine warfare destabilized La Familia, leading to internal strife and fragmentation within the organization.

In the face of mounting pressure, La Familia Michoacana splintered into several factions, each vying for control and influence in a rapidly changing landscape. This fragmentation weakened the cartel's cohesion and operational capacity, but it did not signify the end of its influence. Over the past few years, La Familia has experienced a resurgence in power, re-establishing itself as a notable player in the drug trade. Some factions have regrouped, capitalizing on opportunities presented by the ongoing chaos in the region to reclaim lost territory and reassert their influence.

Today, La Familia Michoacana remains a significant force in the Mexican drug landscape, though it faces ongoing challenges from rival organizations and concerted law enforcement efforts. The cartel's ability to adapt and evolve in response to these challenges is indicative of its resilience. Its operations continue to be heavily centered on methamphetamine production, with established routes into the United States still in place. The resurgence of La Familia has prompted renewed attention from both Mexican authorities and U.S. law enforcement, as they seek to dismantle the cartel's operations and disrupt its growing influence.

As La Familia Michoacana navigates the complexities of the contemporary drug trade, its legacy of violence and community involvement remains a central theme. The cartel's unique approach—combining brutal enforcement tactics with community engagement—reflects the ongoing challenges faced by law enforcement in addressing the multifaceted nature of organized crime. The organization continues to thrive in a landscape fraught with competition, constantly adapting its strategies to maintain relevance in an increasingly volatile environment. The story of La Familia Michoacana serves as a poignant reminder of the intricate interplay between power, ideology, and violence that characterizes the drug trade in Mexico.

The role of various smaller cartels and gangs within the U.S. drug trade cannot be overlooked. Organizations such as the 18th Street Gang and MS-13 have established themselves as significant players in drug distribution, particularly in urban areas. These gangs often collaborate with larger cartels, serving as street-level distributors while also engaging in other criminal activities, including extortion and human trafficking. Their presence has contributed to increased violence in many American cities, as turf wars and rivalries over drug sales often lead to deadly confrontations.

The influence of these gangs underscores the decentralized nature of the U.S. drug trade, where various organizations, both large and small, interact within a complex web of supply and demand. The proliferation of synthetic drugs, particularly fentanyl, has shifted the dynamics of drug trafficking, with smaller gangs increasingly involved in the distribution of potent substances that can be easily transported and concealed. This trend poses significant challenges for law enforcement, as the interconnectedness of cartels and gangs complicates efforts to disrupt drug trafficking networks.

The interplay between major cartels and local gangs highlights the broader implications of drug trafficking on American society. The violence associated with cartel operations often spills into U.S. communities, creating a pervasive atmosphere of fear and insecurity. The associated crime rates increase, leading to heightened tensions between law enforcement and communities grappling with the impacts of addiction and drug-related violence. Efforts to combat drug trafficking must consider the multifaceted nature of the issue, addressing both the supply chains controlled by major cartels and the local dynamics shaped by street-level gangs.

The response to the power of these cartels has evolved alongside the dynamics of the drug trade. Law enforcement agencies in the United States and Mexico have increasingly focused on collaborative efforts to dismantle cartel operations. Initiatives like Operation Intercept and the Mérida Initiative have aimed to strengthen border security and improve intelligence sharing between countries. However, these efforts have faced significant challenges due to the entrenched corruption within law enforcement and political institutions, which often undermines anti-drug strategies.

The U.S. government has also sought to combat drug trafficking through various means, including enhanced law enforcement and interdiction efforts, as well as community-based programs aimed at addressing addiction. These initiatives reflect a growing recognition of the need for a comprehensive approach that balances enforcement with treatment and prevention strategies. While law enforcement efforts have focused on arresting high-profile cartel leaders, there is a growing understanding that sustainable solutions require addressing the root causes of drug demand and the socio-economic factors that contribute to drug trafficking.

The evolution of the major cartels involved in the U.S. drug trade demonstrates the complexities of addressing the issue of drug trafficking. From the historical foundations laid by early organizations like the Sinaloa Cartel to the emergence of powerful entities like the CJNG, the drug trade has continuously adapted to shifting dynamics. Each cartel's operational strategies, territorial disputes, and interactions with law enforcement have shaped the landscape of drug trafficking in the United States. As the drug crisis continues to evolve, understanding the role of these cartels and their impact on society remains crucial in developing effective responses to combat the ongoing challenges posed by drug trafficking and addiction.

The intricate web of routes and networks used to transport drugs into the United States represents a complex and evolving landscape driven by demand, geography, and the relentless pursuit of profit. Drug trafficking organizations (DTOs) have developed sophisticated methods to smuggle an array of substances across the U.S.-Mexico border, leveraging both established pathways and innovative tactics to evade law enforcement.

The U.S.-Mexico border, stretching nearly 2,000 miles, serves as the primary corridor for drug smuggling. This border region is characterized by varied terrain, including deserts, mountains, and urban areas, all of which present unique challenges and opportunities for traffickers. Major entry points have emerged as critical hubs for smuggling operations, including cities like Tijuana, Nogales, and Ciudad Juárez. These locations are strategically chosen due to their proximity to major U.S. cities, facilitating the rapid distribution of drugs across the country.

One of the most notable aspects of drug trafficking into the U.S. is the reliance on established smuggling routes known as "drug corridors."

These corridors have developed over decades, shaped by the dynamics of the drug trade and the responses of law enforcement. For instance, the "Arizona corridor" has become increasingly important for traffickers as they seek alternative routes to evade detection. This corridor allows traffickers to transport drugs through remote areas, leveraging the vast desert landscapes that provide opportunities for concealment. The challenges of terrain are met with creativity, as traffickers utilize all-terrain vehicles and sophisticated navigation technology to traverse these regions undetected.

Tunnels have emerged as a hallmark of drug smuggling operations, representing one of the most innovative methods employed by traffickers. These subterranean routes are often equipped with lighting, ventilation, and rail systems, facilitating the transportation of large quantities of drugs while minimizing detection. The Sinaloa Cartel has been particularly adept at constructing tunnels that connect Mexican warehouses with U.S. counterparts, allowing for the rapid and discreet transfer of drugs. Authorities have uncovered numerous tunnels over the years, but the persistent ingenuity of traffickers means that many others remain hidden. The existence of these tunnels underscores the lengths to which cartels will go to ensure the flow of drugs into the U.S.

Smuggling methods are not limited to traditional land routes. Waterborne transport has become increasingly prevalent, with traffickers using boats and submarines to evade detection. Semi-submersibles, for example, are vessels that can operate just below the water's surface, making them difficult to detect by radar or aerial surveillance. These vessels can carry massive loads of drugs, often making their way from South America to Central America and then up to Mexico before entering the U.S. market. The use of maritime routes highlights the adaptability of drug traffickers in response to law enforcement strategies.

Air transport has also played a role in drug smuggling, although it is less common due to the heightened scrutiny associated with aviation.

Small aircraft are occasionally used to drop shipments in remote areas near the U.S. border. In these instances, drugs are dropped in pre-determined locations, where ground crews await to retrieve the cargo and continue its transport into the U.S. This method poses significant risks, as law enforcement agencies have improved their aerial surveillance capabilities. However, the allure of rapid transport can still attract traffickers willing to take such risks.

Once drugs enter the United States, distribution networks come into play. These networks are often highly organized and operate at multiple levels. At the local level, street gangs and independent dealers are typically responsible for distributing drugs within communities. These smaller organizations often have established relationships with larger cartels, serving as intermediaries that facilitate the movement of drugs from larger distribution hubs to end users.

Major cities such as Los Angeles, Chicago, and New York serve as critical nodes in the distribution network. Each city has its own unique dynamics, influenced by local demand, competition, and law enforcement presence. For example, Los Angeles serves as a significant entry point for drugs entering from Mexico, and its extensive network of gangs ensures rapid distribution throughout California and beyond. The proximity of the city to the U.S.-Mexico border makes it an ideal location for traffickers looking to quickly move large quantities of drugs into the U.S. market.

Distribution networks are often characterized by their adaptability and resilience. When law enforcement takes down a major distributor, new players quickly emerge to fill the void. This constant turnover reflects the ongoing demand for illicit drugs and the economic incentives driving the drug trade. Additionally, the rise of technology has transformed the way drugs are sold and distributed. Online marketplaces and encrypted communication channels enable traffickers to connect with buyers while minimizing risk. These developments have created new challenges for law enforcement, which must constantly adapt to counter these evolving tactics.

In addition to traditional distribution methods, the drug trade has increasingly utilized logistics companies and shipping services to transport drugs into the U.S. These operations often involve the use of legal cargo shipments, where drugs are concealed among legitimate goods. Cartels have forged relationships with corrupt insiders within shipping companies, allowing them to facilitate the smuggling process. Containers loaded with everyday products such as furniture, electronics, or even agricultural goods can be manipulated to hide significant quantities of drugs, enabling traffickers to bypass conventional security measures at ports of entry.

The role of technology in drug smuggling cannot be overstated. Traffickers have employed advanced technologies to enhance their operations, including GPS devices, drones, and encrypted messaging apps. Drones, for instance, have emerged as a tool for scouting routes, transporting small packages, or even delivering drugs directly to designated locations. This technological integration has provided traffickers with a competitive edge, allowing them to respond swiftly to law enforcement efforts and adapt their methods as needed.

The interplay between demand and supply has a direct impact on the routes and networks employed by drug traffickers. The opioid crisis in the United States, driven largely by the rampant abuse of prescription painkillers and heroin, has created a fertile ground for the trafficking of synthetic opioids such as fentanyl. The Sinaloa Cartel and other organizations have capitalized on this demand by increasing the production of fentanyl and its analogs, leading to a rise in overdose deaths across the country. The cartels have established direct supply lines from China for precursor chemicals, facilitating the synthesis of fentanyl in clandestine laboratories located in Mexico. This shift in focus has altered the dynamics of drug trafficking, as traffickers prioritize high-potency drugs that offer greater profit margins.

While the U.S. government has ramped up efforts to combat drug trafficking through law enforcement initiatives and policy reforms, the adaptability of DTOs remains a significant challenge. Law enforcement agencies have made strides in intercepting drug shipments and dismantling key trafficking organizations, but the sheer scale and complexity of the drug trade make it a persistent threat. Cartels continuously evolve their strategies to counter law enforcement tactics, often employing deception, violence, and corruption to maintain their operations.

The international nature of drug trafficking networks further complicates the landscape. Collaborations between Mexican cartels and Colombian cocaine producers or Asian suppliers of precursor chemicals illustrate the interconnectedness of the global drug trade. These collaborations allow cartels to enhance their operational efficiency and diversify their offerings, ensuring a steady flow of drugs into the U.S. market.

As the drug trafficking landscape continues to evolve, understanding the routes and networks used to transport drugs into the U.S. becomes essential for policymakers and law enforcement. The complex interplay of geography, technology, and demand shapes the strategies employed by traffickers, revealing the multifaceted nature of the drug trade. Addressing the challenges posed by drug trafficking requires a comprehensive approach that considers both enforcement and prevention efforts, as well as a commitment to addressing the underlying factors that drive addiction and demand for illicit substances.

The economics of the drug trade represents a complex interplay of supply, demand, and profit, fundamentally driven by American consumption patterns. The United States, as one of the largest consumers of illegal drugs globally, plays a pivotal role in shaping the operations and strategies of drug trafficking organizations (DTOs) in Mexico and beyond. This insatiable demand creates lucrative markets for cartels, enabling them to sustain their operations and exert influence across borders.

At its core, the drug trade operates on a profit-driven model where cartels seek to maximize returns on investment. The production and trafficking of illegal drugs are inherently risky endeavors, but the potential rewards can be staggering. For instance, the cost of producing synthetic opioids like fentanyl in clandestine labs is relatively low compared to the retail prices they fetch on the street. A kilogram of fentanyl, which can cost as little as a few thousand dollars to manufacture, can be sold in the United States for tens of thousands, if not hundreds of thousands, of dollars, depending on purity and demand. This remarkable profit margin incentivizes cartels to invest heavily in production and distribution networks.

American demand for a variety of illicit substances fuels this cycle of profitability. The opioid crisis, characterized by the widespread abuse of prescription painkillers and the subsequent rise in heroin and fentanyl use, exemplifies how shifts in consumer behavior can directly impact drug trafficking operations. As addiction rates soar, so does the demand for drugs, prompting cartels to adapt their operations to meet this evolving market. This responsiveness underscores the economic principle of supply and demand, where cartels prioritize the production of substances that offer the greatest returns based on current trends.

The dynamics of drug pricing further illustrate the economic landscape of the drug trade. Prices for different drugs fluctuate based on availability, law enforcement pressure, and changes in consumer preferences. Cocaine, for instance, remains a staple product for many cartels, with a complex supply chain that begins in South America. As Colombian producers grow coca plants, they rely on Mexican cartels to transport and distribute the final product into the United States. This collaboration allows for economies of scale, where the expertise of cartels in logistics and distribution enhances overall profitability.

In the face of increased enforcement efforts, cartels have adapted their strategies to maintain profitability. For example, when law enforcement intensifies scrutiny at border crossings, cartels may diversify their methods of transport, employing more sophisticated means such as drones, hidden compartments in vehicles, or even commercial shipping methods. The constant evolution of tactics illustrates the resilience of cartels, driven by the economic imperatives of sustaining their operations.

The role of American demand extends beyond traditional drugs. The rise of synthetic drugs, particularly fentanyl and methamphetamine, reflects a market that is responsive to both consumer preferences and the economic realities of drug production. Fentanyl, with its high potency and low production costs, has become a focal point for many cartels, particularly the Sinaloa and Jalisco New Generation Cartels. By establishing connections with Chinese suppliers for precursor chemicals, cartels can efficiently produce fentanyl and distribute it throughout the U.S. This has resulted in catastrophic consequences for public health, as the ease of production and the potency of the drug have led to unprecedented rates of overdose deaths.

The economic incentives driving cartel activity are also fueled by the vast profits generated from the drug trade, which often spill over into other areas of organized crime. Cartels engage in a range of illicit activities beyond drug trafficking, including extortion, human trafficking, and money laundering. These supplementary revenue streams bolster their operations and enable them to exert control over regions, perpetuating cycles of violence and corruption. The intertwining of drug trafficking with other criminal enterprises reflects a broader economic landscape in which cartels operate with relative impunity, often infiltrating legitimate businesses and local economies.

Additionally, the financial resources generated by drug trafficking have profound implications for governance and law enforcement in both the U.S. and Mexico. Corruption often flourishes in regions where cartels operate, as they seek to secure protection from law enforcement and influence political structures. This corruption undermines efforts to combat drug trafficking and disrupts the rule of law, creating a feedback loop that further entrenches the power of cartels. In many cases, local communities become caught in the crossfire, as the violence and instability stemming from cartel activity directly impact public safety and quality of life.

The economic impact of the drug trade is not limited to the profits earned by cartels; it extends to broader societal costs. The U.S. government spends billions annually on law enforcement efforts aimed at combating drug trafficking and its associated violence. The toll of addiction on individuals and families creates additional economic burdens in terms of healthcare costs, lost productivity, and the strain on social services. This multifaceted economic landscape highlights the urgent need for comprehensive solutions that address not only the symptoms of drug trafficking but also the underlying factors driving demand.

Addressing the economics of the drug trade requires a nuanced understanding of the role of American demand in fueling cartel activity. Policymakers must recognize that simply increasing law enforcement efforts is insufficient to combat the complexities of the drug trade. A comprehensive approach that encompasses prevention, treatment, and harm reduction strategies is essential to mitigate demand and ultimately disrupt the economic incentives that sustain cartels. By addressing addiction as a public health issue rather than solely a criminal justice problem, stakeholders can work towards a more sustainable solution that reduces the overall demand for illicit drugs.

The relationship between American demand and cartel activity is deeply intertwined, revealing the economic forces at play in the drug trade. As long as there is a market for illegal substances, cartels will continue to adapt and innovate in their methods of production and distribution. Understanding this dynamic is critical for developing effective strategies to combat drug trafficking and address the root causes of addiction, paving the way for a safer and healthier future.

The economic landscape of the drug trade is fundamentally driven by American demand, which fuels the operations of drug trafficking organizations. This relationship highlights the significant profit margins associated with the production and distribution of illegal substances, particularly synthetic drugs like fentanyl. As demand fluctuates, cartels adapt their strategies to maintain profitability, often diversifying their operations and engaging in a range of criminal activities. The interplay between supply and demand creates a complex environment that challenges law enforcement efforts and perpetuates cycles of violence and corruption. Addressing this multifaceted issue requires a comprehensive approach that tackles addiction as a public health crisis, seeking to reduce demand and disrupt the economic incentives that sustain the drug trade.

The Rise of Fentanyl and Synthetic Drugs

In the shadows of the opioid epidemic, a silent predator lurks, claiming lives at an alarming rate—fentanyl. This synthetic opioid, initially heralded for its powerful pain-relieving properties, has morphed into a lethal force that drives the darkest chapters of America's drug crisis. As the pharmaceutical industry grappled with its over-prescription of opioids, fentanyl slipped into the illicit drug market, fueling addiction and overdose deaths across the nation. The statistics are staggering; every day, hundreds of lives are cut short, families are torn apart, and communities are left grappling with the aftermath of a substance so potent that a mere grain can be fatal. This chapter delves into the rise of fentanyl and other synthetic opioids, exploring how they infiltrated the streets and transformed the landscape of drug abuse, forever altering the lives of those who encounter their deadly grip.

Fentanyl, a synthetic opioid, has emerged as a major player in the ongoing drug crisis in the United States. Originally developed in the 1960s as a potent pain reliever for medical use, fentanyl's unique chemical properties and high potency have made it a double-edged sword. While it provides effective relief for patients suffering from severe pain, its potential for misuse and overdose has led to devastating consequences. Fentanyl is estimated to be 50 to 100 times more potent than morphine and about 50 times more potent than heroin. This incredible strength means that even a minuscule amount can result in a powerful effect, making it both a valuable medical tool and a perilous substance in the hands of those seeking to exploit its effects.

The production of fentanyl involves synthetic processes that allow for the creation of this opioid in a laboratory setting. Unlike natural opioids derived from opium poppies, synthetic opioids can be manufactured using readily available precursors and chemicals. This ease of production is one of the reasons why fentanyl and its analogs have flooded the illicit drug market. Many drug trafficking organizations (DTOs) have shifted their focus toward synthetic opioids due to their profitability and the relatively low cost of production. Fentanyl can be produced in clandestine laboratories, often with little oversight, and distributed through established drug trafficking routes, which has made it an attractive option for cartels looking to increase their market share in the U.S. drug trade.

Fentanyl is often mixed with other drugs, including heroin, cocaine, and counterfeit prescription pills, to enhance potency or reduce production costs. This adulteration has been a significant factor in the rising rates of overdose deaths across the United States. Users often unknowingly consume fentanyl-laced substances, leading to fatal consequences, as they may not be aware of the drug's presence or its potency. The rise of counterfeit pills, often made to resemble legitimate prescription medications, has further exacerbated the crisis, as they can be marketed and sold with little regard for user safety.

The emergence of fentanyl has sparked concern among public health officials and law enforcement alike. The opioid epidemic, which initially began with the over-prescription of opioid painkillers, has evolved into a more complex crisis with the introduction of synthetic opioids. Fentanyl has significantly contributed to the skyrocketing number of overdose deaths in the U.S., with thousands of lives lost each year. According to the Centers for Disease Control and Prevention (CDC), synthetic opioids, primarily fentanyl, accounted for nearly 75% of all opioid-related deaths in 2021. This alarming statistic underscores the need for comprehensive strategies to combat the fentanyl crisis, as its rapid proliferation has far-reaching implications for public health and safety.

Fentanyl's presence on the black market has led to the creation of numerous analogs—modified versions of the drug designed to evade law enforcement detection. These analogs can vary in potency and effects, posing additional risks to users. For instance, drugs like carfentanil, which is intended for use as a tranquilizer for large animals, are even more potent than fentanyl and have been linked to a rise in overdose cases. The development of these analogs illustrates the ongoing battle between drug traffickers and authorities, as new synthetic opioids emerge in response to regulatory efforts to control existing substances.

The rise of synthetic drugs like fentanyl is also attributed to changes in consumer behavior and preferences. Many individuals seeking relief from chronic pain or recreational drug users are drawn to opioids due to their euphoric effects. As prescription opioids have become more tightly regulated, individuals have increasingly turned to illicit alternatives, including fentanyl. The increased availability and accessibility of synthetic opioids have facilitated this transition, allowing users to acquire potent substances without the need for a prescription.

Law enforcement agencies face significant challenges in combating the influx of fentanyl and other synthetic opioids. The drug's small size and potency make it difficult to detect and intercept, even at points of entry like borders and ports. Additionally, the rapid production and distribution capabilities of DTOs complicate efforts to dismantle their operations. Law enforcement must navigate a complex landscape where synthetic opioids are produced in one country, trafficked through another, and consumed in a third, necessitating international cooperation and coordination.

The health impacts of fentanyl and synthetic opioids extend beyond immediate overdose risks. The opioid crisis has strained healthcare systems across the country, as emergency departments grapple with the influx of overdose cases and the need for addiction treatment services. The social implications are equally dire, as families and communities bear the brunt of the consequences associated with opioid misuse. The trauma of losing a loved one to overdose can have lasting effects on individuals and communities, perpetuating cycles of grief and despair.

Efforts to address the fentanyl crisis have included increasing public awareness, expanding access to treatment, and implementing harm reduction strategies. Initiatives such as the distribution of naloxone, an opioid overdose reversal medication, aim to reduce the number of fatal overdoses. Naloxone can quickly restore breathing in individuals experiencing an opioid overdose, offering a critical lifeline in emergency situations. Education campaigns aimed at informing the public about the dangers of fentanyl and the risks associated with counterfeit drugs are also essential components of a comprehensive response.

Pharmaceutical companies and healthcare providers are now under scrutiny for their role in the opioid crisis. The over-prescription of opioid medications in the past laid the groundwork for the current epidemic. Addressing the root causes of opioid misuse and implementing responsible prescribing practices is crucial for preventing future addiction and overdose cases. Additionally, mental health support and addiction treatment services must be accessible to those struggling with substance use disorders, as many individuals may turn to opioids as a means of coping with underlying issues such as trauma or mental illness.

The evolution of fentanyl and other synthetic opioids reflects broader trends in drug use and trafficking, illustrating the challenges faced by individuals, communities, and authorities. The increasing complexity of the opioid crisis necessitates a multifaceted approach that encompasses prevention, treatment, and harm reduction.

Understanding the dynamics of fentanyl and its role in the drug trade is essential for developing effective strategies to combat its proliferation and mitigate its impact on public health.

Fentanyl's rise in popularity has also sparked significant discussion about drug policy and regulation. Many advocates argue for a re-evaluation of current approaches to drug enforcement, emphasizing the need for a public health-centered framework that prioritizes harm reduction over punitive measures. By focusing on treatment and prevention, society can address the root causes of addiction while minimizing the stigma associated with substance use disorders.

The increasing availability of synthetic opioids underscores the importance of ongoing research into addiction, pain management, and drug policy. Policymakers must remain informed about emerging trends in the drug landscape, ensuring that responses are adaptable to new challenges. This includes promoting evidence-based strategies for prevention, treatment, and recovery, as well as fostering collaboration between public health agencies, law enforcement, and community organizations.

As the fentanyl crisis continues to unfold, its implications for public health, safety, and policy cannot be overstated. The need for a comprehensive response that incorporates prevention, treatment, harm reduction, and education is paramount in addressing the challenges posed by synthetic opioids. Acknowledging the complexity of the opioid crisis and fostering collaboration among stakeholders will be essential in navigating this pressing public health issue and mitigating the impact of fentanyl and other synthetic drugs on individuals and communities across the United States.

The ongoing evolution of fentanyl and synthetic opioids presents a formidable challenge for society. Understanding the unique characteristics of these substances and their effects on individuals and communities is crucial for developing effective strategies to combat the crisis. By prioritizing public health and adopting a holistic approach to addiction and substance use, society can work toward a future where individuals are supported in their recovery journeys, reducing the devastating toll of fentanyl and synthetic drugs on lives and communities.

The emergence of fentanyl-laced drugs has reshaped the landscape of substance abuse, thrusting countless individuals into a perilous game where the stakes are life and death. Fentanyl, a synthetic opioid 50 to 100 times more potent than morphine, has found its way into an alarming array of street drugs. Users seeking the euphoria of heroin or the stimulating effects of cocaine may unknowingly consume a product laced with this deadly substance. The consequences are often devastating, as even a minuscule amount of fentanyl can lead to fatal overdoses.

The prevalence of fentanyl in the drug supply marks a significant departure from the traditional patterns of substance abuse. Previously, drug users could often gauge the strength and effects of their chosen substances. With fentanyl's incorporation into the mix, however, users face an unpredictable landscape. A single pill or a small bag of powder may contain lethal doses of fentanyl, turning a routine high into a catastrophic event. The danger is exacerbated by the increasing sophistication of counterfeit pills, which mimic legitimate pharmaceuticals but are infused with fentanyl. Users, particularly those seeking pain relief or recreational experiences, often have no way of knowing the true contents of what they are consuming.

Fentanyl's rapid onset and high potency make it especially dangerous. When ingested, it floods the brain's opioid receptors, leading to feelings of intense euphoria. This swift action can quickly transition to respiratory depression, where the body's ability to breathe is severely impaired. Many users may not recognize the onset of overdose until it is too late, as the effects can manifest suddenly and violently. The statistics are grim; fentanyl-related overdose deaths have surged, eclipsing previous records and contributing to the larger opioid crisis that has gripped the United States.

Communities across the country are grappling with the fallout from this crisis. Families are torn apart as loved ones succumb to addiction and overdose, and friends are left to mourn those they have lost. The emotional and psychological toll of fentanyl-laced drugs extends far beyond the individual, affecting entire communities and straining local resources. Emergency services are inundated with calls related to overdoses, and hospitals find themselves on the front lines of a battle against an ever-increasing tide of fentanyl-related emergencies.

The role of fentanyl in the overdose crisis is further complicated by its intersection with mental health issues and socioeconomic factors. Individuals grappling with trauma, anxiety, or depression may turn to drugs as a coping mechanism, unknowingly putting themselves at risk for encountering fentanyl-laced substances. The stigma surrounding addiction often prevents individuals from seeking help, trapping them in a cycle of dependence that can lead to devastating outcomes. In many cases, the very substances that provide temporary relief can ultimately become instruments of their demise.

Law enforcement agencies and public health officials are grappling with how to address this evolving crisis. Strategies aimed at harm reduction are gaining traction, emphasizing the importance of education and access to lifesaving interventions like naloxone. This medication can reverse the effects of an opioid overdose, providing a critical window of opportunity for those who have fallen victim to fentanyl. However, the efficacy of these measures is often hindered by the rapid pace at which fentanyl is infiltrating the drug supply.

In response to the escalating crisis, communities are increasingly mobilizing to create awareness campaigns that educate users about the dangers of fentanyl-laced drugs. These initiatives aim to disseminate information about recognizing the signs of overdose and the availability of naloxone, equipping individuals with the tools necessary to respond in emergencies. Yet, despite these efforts, the pervasive nature of fentanyl continues to pose significant challenges.

The unpredictability of the drug supply has created an atmosphere of fear and uncertainty among users, who may feel compelled to continue using while simultaneously recognizing the heightened risks. This paradox highlights the complexities of addiction, where the compulsion to use often overrides rational decision-making. Many users feel trapped, aware of the dangers yet unable to break free from the grip of substance dependence.

Fentanyl's role in the overdose crisis underscores the urgent need for comprehensive solutions that address the root causes of addiction while also providing immediate support for those in crisis. Treatment options must be expanded to include a spectrum of services, from medically-assisted treatment to mental health support. Community-based approaches that prioritize empathy and understanding can help bridge the gap between those struggling with addiction and the resources they need to recover.

As fentanyl-laced drugs continue to permeate the drug landscape, the implications for public health are staggering. The healthcare system is stretched thin, grappling with the overwhelming number of overdose cases and the long-term effects of opioid addiction. Addressing the crisis requires a multifaceted approach, with collaboration between law enforcement, healthcare providers, and community organizations.

This chapter aims to illuminate the dangerous interplay between fentanyl-laced drugs and the broader overdose crisis, shedding light on the urgent need for a collective response. Understanding the nuances of this issue is crucial for developing effective strategies to combat the epidemic and provide support for those affected by addiction. As communities strive to reclaim their neighborhoods from the grips of addiction, it is imperative to foster an environment of understanding, compassion, and resilience in the face of this daunting challenge.

Fentanyl and its analogs have irrevocably changed the narrative of drug use in America. The next steps in addressing this crisis must prioritize education, prevention, and treatment, ensuring that individuals struggling with addiction are met with the support they need to heal and rebuild their lives. Together, communities can forge a path forward, navigating the complexities of the synthetic opioid epidemic while advocating for change and hope in the face of despair.

Fentanyl has irrevocably altered the landscape of drug use in America, creating a crisis that transcends previous patterns of substance abuse. The introduction of this potent synthetic opioid into the drug market marked a significant turning point, one that has transformed not only the substances being abused but also the demographics of those affected, the nature of addiction, and the strategies needed for intervention and recovery.

Initially, opioid abuse in the United States largely revolved around prescription painkillers, with drugs like oxycodone and hydrocodone dominating the scene. The pharmaceutical industry's aggressive marketing of these medications in the late 1990s led to widespread overprescription and misuse, paving the way for an opioid epidemic. However, as prescription regulations tightened and the availability of prescription opioids diminished, many users turned to the black market. It was in this environment that fentanyl began to emerge, both as a legitimate medical treatment for severe pain and as a dangerous illicit substance.

Fentanyl's potency, which can be 50 to 100 times greater than that of morphine, has made it an attractive option for drug traffickers seeking to maximize profits. This led to the introduction of fentanyl in various forms, from powder to counterfeit pills designed to mimic legitimate medications. Users, often unaware of the presence of fentanyl, unwittingly put themselves at risk by consuming these laced products. The result has been a shocking surge in overdose deaths, particularly among those who may have previously engaged in recreational drug use without facing life-threatening risks.

The demographic of drug users has shifted dramatically in response to the proliferation of fentanyl. While traditional notions of addiction often conjure images of marginalized individuals, the reality is that fentanyl has infiltrated communities across socioeconomic boundaries. Young adults, college students, and even those in professional environments have been impacted, highlighting that addiction is a complex issue that does not discriminate based on social status.

Fentanyl's rise has also brought about a change in the nature of addiction itself. The intensity of the high it produces, combined with its rapid onset, creates a cycle of use that can quickly escalate. Many individuals find themselves trapped in a cycle of dependence, with the need for immediate relief driving them to seek out increasingly potent drugs. This has led to an increase in poly-substance use, where individuals combine fentanyl with other drugs, further compounding the dangers associated with each substance. For instance, users might mix fentanyl with stimulants like cocaine or methamphetamine, seeking to enhance the euphoric effects, but this practice can have lethal consequences.

The stigma surrounding addiction has also intensified, as the dangers associated with fentanyl-laced drugs have prompted fear and misunderstanding. Families and communities grappling with the realities of fentanyl addiction may find themselves at a loss, often unsure of how to address the issue or support their loved ones. The resulting isolation can exacerbate the challenges faced by those struggling with addiction, making it even harder for them to seek help.

Moreover, the public health response to the fentanyl crisis has evolved in tandem with its rise. Health officials are increasingly recognizing the need for harm reduction strategies, focusing not only on prevention and treatment but also on minimizing the immediate dangers associated with fentanyl use. Initiatives such as the distribution of naloxone, a life-saving medication that can reverse opioid overdoses, have become more widespread. These efforts aim to empower communities and individuals with the tools needed to respond effectively to overdose situations, potentially saving countless lives.

Law enforcement agencies, too, have been forced to adapt their strategies in response to fentanyl's impact. The increasing presence of synthetic opioids in the drug supply has led to intensified efforts to disrupt trafficking networks and curb the distribution of these dangerous substances. However, the rapid pace at which fentanyl is produced and distributed poses significant challenges for authorities. The ongoing battle between law enforcement and drug traffickers has led to a continuous cat-and-mouse game, where cartels and organizations find ways to circumvent restrictions and regulations.

The fentanyl crisis has highlighted the need for comprehensive drug policy reform. As the situation evolves, there is a growing recognition that punitive measures alone are insufficient to address the complexities of addiction and drug use. Many advocates are calling for a shift towards a public health-oriented approach, one that prioritizes treatment, education, and support over criminalization. This shift recognizes that addiction is often rooted in trauma, mental health issues, and socioeconomic factors, necessitating a multifaceted response that addresses these underlying causes.

In addition to changing public health strategies, the fentanyl crisis has also spurred conversations about the importance of community engagement. Grassroots organizations, often led by those with lived experiences of addiction, are emerging as vital players in the fight against fentanyl. These groups work to raise awareness, provide education, and offer support to individuals and families affected by addiction. By fostering connections within communities, they aim to break down the stigma surrounding drug use and create environments where individuals feel safe seeking help.

As fentanyl continues to permeate the drug landscape, the implications for American society are profound. The epidemic has exposed the cracks in existing systems, revealing the urgent need for comprehensive solutions that prioritize empathy, understanding, and healing. The sheer magnitude of the crisis necessitates a collective response, where healthcare providers, law enforcement, community organizations, and individuals come together to confront the challenges posed by fentanyl and other synthetic opioids.

Ultimately, fentanyl's impact on the landscape of drug use in America serves as a stark reminder of the complexities surrounding addiction and the need for informed, compassionate responses. The narrative of drug use has shifted, and in order to effectively address the crisis, society must adapt to this new reality. By prioritizing education, prevention, and treatment, communities can forge a path forward, ensuring that individuals struggling with addiction are met with the support and resources they need to reclaim their lives. In doing so, the hope remains that a brighter future can be built—one that moves beyond the shadows of fentanyl and embraces healing, recovery, and resilience.

The rise of fentanyl and other synthetic opioids marks a critical juncture in the ongoing battle against drug abuse and addiction. As these substances are manufactured in clandestine labs, their distribution has become alarmingly sophisticated, with traffickers using advanced techniques to conceal and transport these deadly drugs. Often mixed with other substances, fentanyl-laced products are now commonplace in the illicit drug market, placing users at a heightened risk of overdose without their knowledge. The sheer potency of fentanyl has dramatically escalated the overdose crisis, leading to an unprecedented number of deaths across diverse communities.

This evolving landscape of drug use in America is a stark reminder of the complexities of addiction. Once viewed through the lens of traditional opioids, the current reality demands a reevaluation of our understanding of substance abuse, public health responses, and community support systems. The integration of fentanyl into the drug supply has not only transformed the types of substances being used but has also reshaped the demographics of those affected, requiring a comprehensive approach that prioritizes education, harm reduction, and compassionate treatment. As the crisis continues to unfold, the imperative to address these challenges with urgency and empathy has never been clearer, highlighting the need for a collective commitment to combat the devastating impact of synthetic opioids.

Commonly Abused Drugs and Their Impact

The landscape of substance abuse is vast and ever-changing, shaped by cultural, social, and economic factors that influence patterns of drug use across generations. While the opioid epidemic has captured much of the national attention in recent years, a diverse array of substances continues to pose significant threats to public health and safety. From stimulants like cocaine and methamphetamine to depressants such as alcohol and benzodiazepines, each drug brings its own unique set of challenges, consequences, and complexities. Understanding these commonly abused drugs is crucial for grasping their impact on individuals, families, and communities.

The repercussions of drug abuse extend far beyond the individual user, rippling through society in the form of increased crime rates, healthcare costs, and lost productivity. Communities bear the burden of dealing with the fallout from addiction, which often includes strained relationships, economic instability, and a heightened risk of overdose. As we delve into the world of commonly abused drugs, we will explore their origins, effects, and the multifaceted consequences of their misuse, shedding light on the urgent need for comprehensive prevention and treatment strategies. Through this examination, we aim to foster a deeper understanding of the pervasive influence these substances have on the fabric of society and the lives they touch.

The grip of addiction has tightened across the United States, transforming lives, families, and entire communities. Amid this ongoing crisis, four primary substances stand out: heroin, methamphetamine, cocaine, and prescription opioids. Each drug weaves a complex narrative of dependency, destruction, and the relentless pursuit of relief that entraps millions. Understanding these substances is crucial in unraveling the larger story of addiction in America—a story marked by suffering, resilience, and the urgent need for effective responses.

Heroin, an illicit opioid, casts a long shadow over the landscape of addiction. Derived from morphine, which is extracted from the opium poppy, heroin is notorious for its potency and addictive properties. Initially celebrated for its pain-relieving effects, it quickly evolved into a drug associated with despair and tragedy. Users often seek heroin to escape the harsh realities of life, finding temporary solace in the drug's euphoric high. The allure of heroin lies in its ability to induce intense feelings of pleasure and relaxation, but this comes at a steep price. The journey from casual use to full-blown addiction can occur rapidly, with many users finding themselves trapped in a cycle of dependency within just a few short months.

The methods of heroin consumption further complicate its dangers. Users often inject, snort, or smoke the drug, each method carrying its own risks. Injection, while providing the quickest and most intense high, significantly increases the risk of overdose and the spread of infectious diseases like HIV and hepatitis. The potency of heroin can vary widely, particularly as it is often cut with other substances to increase profits. In recent years, the dangerous trend of mixing heroin with synthetic opioids like fentanyl has led to a staggering increase in overdose deaths. Users, often unaware of the presence of fentanyl, may take a dose they believe to be safe only to be met with a life-threatening reaction. The tragic irony is that many individuals who turn to heroin do so as an escape from pain, only to find themselves facing a more profound and life-threatening struggle.

The rise of methamphetamine represents another chapter in the evolving narrative of substance abuse. Originally synthesized for medical use in the early 20th century, meth has transformed into a powerful and highly addictive illicit drug. Methamphetamine's crystal form, often referred to as "crystal meth," has gained notoriety for its intense and euphoric effects, attracting users from diverse backgrounds. Unlike heroin, which offers sedation, methamphetamine stimulates the central nervous system, leading to increased energy, alertness, and feelings of euphoria. However, the high is fleeting, prompting users to consume more in rapid succession. This cycle of use can quickly lead to severe physical and psychological dependence.

Manufactured in clandestine labs, meth is often produced in unsanitary conditions using toxic chemicals. The drug can be ingested through various methods, including smoking, snorting, or injecting. Each method carries inherent risks, with smoking or injecting providing the most intense high while also increasing the likelihood of addiction. The physical toll of methamphetamine use is staggering, leading to a range of health issues, including severe dental problems often referred to as "meth mouth," cardiovascular complications, and significant weight loss. Psychologically, users may experience paranoia, anxiety, and violent behavior, creating a cycle of destruction that extends beyond the individual.

Cocaine, a stimulant derived from the coca plant, has long been a staple in the realm of illicit substances. The euphoric rush produced by cocaine is highly sought after, drawing users into a pattern of abuse that can quickly spiral out of control. Available in both powdered and crack forms, cocaine is often consumed through snorting or smoking, with each method delivering a rapid onset of effects. The drug's ability to create intense feelings of euphoria and increased energy comes at a cost, as the high is short-lived, leading users to seek repeated doses in a relentless pursuit of pleasure.

Cocaine's impact on health is significant, with users facing serious risks, including cardiovascular issues, respiratory problems, and neurological complications. The psychological effects of cocaine use can be equally damaging, leading to anxiety, paranoia, and depression. The drug's allure, coupled with its potential for addiction, has made it a pervasive presence in American culture. It has infiltrated social scenes, contributing to a rise in substance-related incidents, violence, and crime. The social implications of cocaine use extend beyond the individual, impacting families and communities as the consequences of addiction ripple through lives.

Prescription opioids, initially developed as legitimate pain management solutions, have become a central focus of the ongoing opioid crisis. Medications such as oxycodone, hydrocodone, and morphine, once viewed as breakthroughs in pain relief, have unleashed a wave of addiction that has devastated countless lives. Aggressive marketing and overprescription led to widespread availability, and many individuals began using these medications for legitimate medical reasons, only to find themselves trapped in a cycle of dependency. The transition from prescription opioids to illicit drugs, such as heroin or fentanyl, is alarmingly common, as individuals seek to maintain their high or escape the withdrawal symptoms associated with stopping their prescribed medications.

The consequences of prescription opioid abuse extend far beyond individual users. Families bear the burden of loved ones trapped in addiction, facing the emotional toll of watching someone they care about struggle with dependency. Communities grapple with the broader implications of addiction, including increased healthcare costs, the strain on law enforcement, and the loss of productivity. The tragic reality is that prescription opioids, once seen as a solution to pain, have become a catalyst for a national health crisis.

The interplay between these commonly abused drugs reveals a complex web of addiction, social impact, and health consequences. Each substance tells a story of human vulnerability, resilience, and the desperate pursuit of relief from pain, whether physical or emotional. Addressing the crisis requires a multifaceted approach that goes beyond individual treatment to encompass prevention, education, and community support. Understanding the nuances of heroin, methamphetamine, cocaine, and prescription opioids is essential to developing effective strategies to combat the pervasive drug epidemic gripping the nation.

This ongoing battle against addiction highlights the urgent need for comprehensive responses that address the root causes of substance abuse. The convergence of these drugs creates a volatile environment in which individuals may find themselves trapped in a cycle of dependency, often without the support or resources needed to break free. As society grapples with the implications of addiction, it becomes increasingly clear that addressing the crisis requires a collective effort from healthcare providers, law enforcement, policymakers, and communities.

Recognizing the unique characteristics and challenges associated with each substance is crucial in devising effective strategies for prevention and intervention. By fostering a greater understanding of the landscape of substance abuse, we can work towards developing tailored solutions that address the needs of individuals and communities alike. In this fight against addiction, knowledge and awareness serve as powerful tools for change, offering hope for a future where individuals can find recovery and reclaim their lives from the clutches of substance abuse.

The landscape of substance abuse is marked not only by the prevalence of various drugs but also by the unique dangers and addictive qualities each substance possesses. While the allure of heroin, methamphetamine, cocaine, and prescription opioids may draw individuals into their grasp, it is the specific characteristics of these drugs that often lead to devastating consequences. Understanding these unique dangers and the factors that contribute to their addictive qualities is essential in addressing the ongoing crisis of addiction in the United States.

Heroin's potency is one of its most dangerous attributes. As an opioid, heroin binds to the brain's opioid receptors, which are involved in pain perception and reward. This binding results in an immediate release of dopamine, creating feelings of euphoria. The speed at which heroin reaches the brain plays a crucial role in its addictive potential. Users often describe the high as "a rush," with effects that can be intensely pleasurable. However, the rapid onset of these effects is closely tied to the potential for overdose. The margin between a safe dose and a lethal dose can be incredibly slim, especially when users are unaware of the drug's purity or the presence of other substances like fentanyl.

The method of consumption further amplifies the risks associated with heroin use. Injection, for example, allows the drug to enter the bloodstream almost instantaneously, producing a powerful high that can lead to repeated use in a short time frame. This urgency to experience the high again increases the likelihood of developing a tolerance, meaning users need to consume more of the drug to achieve the same effects. Over time, the body becomes reliant on heroin, leading to physical dependence and withdrawal symptoms when not using the drug. This cycle of use and withdrawal is a hallmark of addiction, trapping individuals in a downward spiral that is difficult to escape.

Methamphetamine, known for its intense stimulant effects, presents its own set of unique dangers. The drug increases the release of dopamine, leading to heightened energy, alertness, and an overwhelming sense of pleasure. The psychological effects can be enticing, with users often experiencing increased confidence and sociability. However, the high from methamphetamine is notoriously short-lived, typically lasting only a few hours, which prompts users to consume more to maintain the desired effects. This pattern of repeated use can rapidly escalate into addiction.

Methamphetamine's impact on the body and mind can be devastating. The drug can cause significant cardiovascular strain, leading to increased heart rates, high blood pressure, and potential heart failure. Additionally, the psychological effects can result in severe anxiety, paranoia, and hallucinations. Chronic use can lead to a condition known as "meth-induced psychosis," where users may experience delusions and severe mood swings. This psychological turmoil not only affects the user but can also lead to violent behavior, endangering those around them and contributing to a broader cycle of crime and instability.

Cocaine, another potent stimulant, carries its own dangers rooted in its addictive qualities. The drug works by inhibiting the reuptake of dopamine, leading to an accumulation of this neurotransmitter in the brain. The euphoric effects of cocaine are typically felt within minutes, making it a popular choice among users seeking a quick high. However, the intensity of the high is matched by a harsh comedown, often characterized by feelings of fatigue, irritability, and depression. This crash leads many users to seek additional doses, creating a cycle of dependency that can escalate quickly.

Cocaine's addictive nature is compounded by the social settings in which it is often used. Parties and social gatherings can create an environment where users feel pressured to continue using the drug to maintain their high and social status. The stigma surrounding addiction can also deter individuals from seeking help, as they may fear judgment from peers or loved ones. The short-lived effects of cocaine, combined with the societal pressures surrounding its use, contribute to its high potential for addiction and the challenges associated with recovery.

Prescription opioids, despite their initial medical purpose, present unique dangers that have led to widespread addiction. Medications such as oxycodone and hydrocodone are designed to alleviate pain, but their addictive properties can lead individuals down a treacherous path. These drugs bind to the same opioid receptors in the brain as heroin, producing similar feelings of euphoria and pain relief. The risk of addiction often arises from the initial legitimate use of these medications for pain management, creating a situation where individuals inadvertently develop a dependency.

The medical community's response to pain has also played a role in the opioid crisis. In recent decades, there has been a significant push to manage pain more aggressively, leading to increased prescriptions for opioids. Patients, often unaware of the addictive potential of these medications, may find themselves reliant on them to function. The transition from prescribed opioids to illicit substances, such as heroin or fentanyl, is alarmingly common as individuals seek to maintain their high or mitigate withdrawal symptoms. This cycle not only complicates the individual's relationship with substances but also contributes to the broader public health crisis.

Each of these substances presents unique dangers and challenges that require targeted responses to address their impact on individuals and communities. The interplay between addiction, mental health, and social factors must be understood to develop effective prevention and intervention strategies. Acknowledging the specific characteristics and risks associated with heroin, methamphetamine, cocaine, and prescription opioids is essential for policymakers, healthcare providers, and communities striving to combat the pervasive drug epidemic.

Education plays a crucial role in mitigating the dangers of these drugs. Comprehensive drug education programs that inform individuals about the risks associated with each substance can empower people to make informed choices. Such programs should emphasize the potential for addiction, the health risks involved, and the importance of seeking help if one finds themselves struggling with substance use. Early intervention is critical in preventing the escalation of drug use into full-blown addiction, and access to resources and support can make a significant difference.

Moreover, fostering open conversations about addiction and substance use within families and communities can help to reduce stigma and encourage individuals to seek help. Support systems that provide understanding, compassion, and resources for those affected by addiction can create a more conducive environment for recovery. By breaking down the barriers that prevent individuals from reaching out for help, communities can work together to combat the challenges posed by these commonly abused drugs.

Addressing the unique dangers and addictive qualities of heroin, methamphetamine, cocaine, and prescription opioids is an ongoing process that requires collaboration across multiple sectors. Healthcare providers, educators, policymakers, and communities must unite to develop effective strategies for prevention, treatment, and support. By fostering awareness and understanding of these substances, society can begin to dismantle the cycles of addiction and work towards a future where individuals can reclaim their lives from the grip of substance abuse. Through collective efforts, it is possible to turn the tide against the pervasive epidemic of addiction and create a healthier, more supportive environment for those affected.

The health, social, and economic impacts of commonly abused drugs extend far beyond the individual user, permeating families, communities, and even broader societal structures. Heroin, for example, is notorious for its potential to cause fatal overdoses. The drug's potency, particularly when mixed with other substances like fentanyl, heightens the risk of respiratory failure, which can occur within moments of use. Beyond the immediate danger of overdose, chronic heroin use can lead to a host of other health problems, including infectious diseases such as HIV and hepatitis C. These diseases are often spread through shared needles among users, further complicating the public health response. The lifestyle associated with heroin addiction can also lead to poor nutrition, dental problems, and overall deterioration of physical health. Methamphetamine use similarly wreaks havoc on both physical and mental health. Users may experience severe dental issues, commonly referred to as "meth mouth," characterized by tooth decay and gum disease. The drug's stimulant effects can lead to cardiovascular problems, including heart attacks and strokes, particularly with prolonged use. Additionally, methamphetamine is linked to severe mental health disorders. Users often report increased anxiety, paranoia, and even hallucinations, which can result in violent behavior. The mental health implications extend beyond the individual, affecting families and communities as they cope with the unpredictable behaviors of those using the drug. Cocaine, while often glamorized in popular culture, poses its own set of health risks. The drug can lead to cardiovascular issues, including heart attacks and arrhythmias, even in young, otherwise healthy individuals. Cocaine's impact on mental health is significant, with users experiencing heightened anxiety, irritability, and depressive symptoms during withdrawal. This cycle of euphoria followed by a crash exacerbates mental health issues and can lead to a reliance on the drug for temporary relief. Prescription opioids, though initially used for legitimate medical purposes, have spiraled into a crisis of addiction. These drugs can lead to physical dependence, where users require higher doses to achieve the same level of pain relief or euphoria, often resulting in a dangerous cycle of increased use. Opioid addiction can lead to overdose, respiratory depression, and a range of health complications, including the risk of developing comorbid mental health disorders. The opioid epidemic has also placed immense pressure on healthcare systems, with emergency rooms seeing a surge in overdose cases and healthcare providers scrambling to address the growing need for addiction treatment and mental health support. The social impacts of these drugs are equally devastating. Families often bear the brunt of the consequences, with relationships strained by the chaos of addiction. Parents struggling with substance abuse may find it challenging to provide a stable environment for their children, leading to neglect and developmental issues. Children in these situations may experience trauma, which can result in long-term psychological effects and increased risk of substance abuse in their own lives. Communities suffer as well, facing increased crime rates associated with drug trafficking and related violence. Areas heavily affected by substance abuse often see a rise in property crimes, such as theft and burglary, as individuals resort to illegal activities to support their addiction. The stigma surrounding drug use can further alienate individuals and families affected by addiction, discouraging them from seeking help and exacerbating feelings of isolation and hopelessness. Economically, the impact of drug abuse is staggering. The cost of addiction extends beyond the individual, burdening families and communities with financial strain. Healthcare costs associated with treating addiction and its related health complications can quickly accumulate. Employers also face increased absenteeism and decreased productivity due to the effects of substance abuse on their workforce. The economic toll of the opioid epidemic alone has been estimated in the hundreds of billions of dollars, factoring in healthcare costs, lost productivity, and criminal justice expenses. Efforts to combat the drug crisis, including prevention and treatment programs, require significant financial investment from both public and private sectors. However, the potential for positive economic outcomes through effective intervention is substantial. By addressing substance abuse and supporting recovery, communities can reduce the overall economic burden while improving quality of life for individuals and families. In summary, the health, social, and economic impacts of commonly abused drugs like heroin, methamphetamine, cocaine, and prescription opioids are profound and far-reaching. Understanding these consequences is essential for developing effective strategies to address the ongoing drug crisis, support those affected, and foster healthier communities.

The Overdose Crisis

Every day, the headlines scream of an escalating crisis that is claiming lives at an alarming rate—the overdose epidemic. Across the United States, families are shattered, communities are reeling, and the nation is grappling with an unprecedented wave of fatalities linked to drug overdoses. In 2021 alone, over 100,000 people succumbed to this crisis, with synthetic opioids like fentanyl driving the surge. The numbers are not just statistics; they represent fathers, mothers, brothers, sisters—individuals whose potential was cut short in an instant. The overwhelming presence of these potent drugs in our society creates a ticking clock, as users unknowingly gamble with their lives each time they engage in substance use. The urgency of this situation cannot be overstated; we are in the midst of a public health emergency that demands immediate attention and action. As we delve into the complexities of the overdose crisis, it becomes crucial to understand not only the scale of the problem but also the underlying factors contributing to this devastating trend. The time for complacency has long passed; it is now a matter of collective responsibility to confront the overdose epidemic head-on, advocating for change and supporting those affected by this harrowing reality.

The overdose crisis in the United States has spiraled into a catastrophic emergency over the last decade, marked by a staggering rise in drug-related fatalities. Each statistic represents not just a number, but a life cut short, a family shattered, and a community left to pick up the pieces. In 2014, the nation grappled with approximately 47,000 drug overdose deaths. By 2016, that number had soared to nearly 64,000, signaling a critical turning point. The crisis escalated rapidly; by 2019, over 70,000 individuals succumbed to overdoses, and the situation has only worsened since then.

The deadly grip of synthetic opioids, especially fentanyl, has transformed the landscape of drug use in America. This potent substance, often mixed with other drugs without users' knowledge, has driven overdose deaths to unimaginable heights. The year 2020 saw the COVID-19 pandemic exacerbate this already dire situation, culminating in a staggering record of over 93,000 overdose fatalities. Preliminary estimates for 2021 indicate that this horrifying figure has crossed the 100,000 mark, marking a grim milestone in an already devastating epidemic.

Demographic trends reveal the crisis's widening net. Initially, the opioid epidemic largely impacted white, middle-class individuals, but recent statistics tell a different story. Overdose rates among Black and Hispanic communities have surged dramatically, emphasizing the urgent need for targeted intervention strategies. Young adults aged 18 to 25 are particularly at risk, with rising overdose rates signaling a troubling trend among this vulnerable group.

The phenomenon of poly-drug use complicates the narrative further. Increasingly, users are mixing multiple substances, heightening the risk of overdose. The combination of stimulants like cocaine or methamphetamine with opioids has become alarmingly prevalent. In 2021, approximately 60% of all overdose deaths involved synthetic opioids, underscoring fentanyl's pervasive influence in the current drug market. The presence of fentanyl in heroin and counterfeit pills has transformed drug consumption into a perilous gamble, making treatment efforts even more challenging.

Geographically, the crisis's epicenter has shifted over the years. States in the Northeast and Midwest, once seen as the hardest hit, continue to report high overdose rates. However, the crisis is now spreading to Southern states like Florida and Texas, which are witnessing alarming increases in drug-related fatalities. West Virginia, Kentucky, and Ohio consistently report some of the highest overdose rates, but the rise of fentanyl has unleashed a wave of overdose crises across the nation, leaving no region untouched.

The economic implications of this crisis are staggering. Estimates suggest that drug overdoses cost the U.S. economy over $600 billion annually, encompassing healthcare expenses, lost productivity, and burdens on the criminal justice system. Tackling this crisis through effective prevention and treatment strategies could save significant amounts of money while benefiting society at large.

In response to the overdose epidemic, a multifaceted approach has emerged. Increasing access to addiction treatment and harm reduction services is now a top priority. The introduction of naloxone, an opioid overdose reversal drug, has been a lifeline for countless individuals, enabling immediate action during overdose events. Communities are adopting harm reduction strategies such as syringe exchange programs and supervised consumption sites to mitigate risks associated with drug use.

Despite these efforts, formidable challenges remain. Stigma surrounding addiction continues to hinder individuals from seeking help, creating barriers that prevent many from accessing the treatment they need. Access to addiction services remains uneven, particularly in marginalized communities, leaving many without the necessary support. The drug supply continues to evolve, with new synthetic opioids emerging at an alarming rate, demanding that public health responses remain agile and adaptive.

The stark statistics and trends related to drug overdoses paint a grim picture of a nation in crisis. The dramatic rise in fatalities linked to synthetic opioids, particularly fentanyl, underscores the urgent need for a comprehensive response to this epidemic. Understanding these trends is crucial for crafting effective strategies that address the complex realities of the overdose crisis. This multifaceted challenge requires a collective commitment to prevention, treatment, and support for those grappling with substance use disorders. The time for action is now, as the toll of this crisis continues to rise, demanding immediate and sustained attention from every corner of society.

As of 2024, the drug overdose crisis in the United States remains alarming, with fentanyl being a major contributor to this public health emergency. Recent statistics indicate that overdose deaths have continued to rise, with a significant portion attributed to synthetic opioids, particularly fentanyl. In 2022, nearly 70% of overdose deaths involved fentanyl, which is increasingly found in combination with other drugs, heightening the risk of fatal outcomes.

From 2012 to 2021, there was a staggering increase in drug overdose deaths, reaching over 107,000 fatalities in 2021 alone, and preliminary data for 2022 shows that this trend has unfortunately continued. Fentanyl-related overdose deaths have seen exponential growth, with synthetic opioids (excluding methadone) accounting for nearly 71,000 of those deaths. The demographic most affected includes adults aged 26 to 39, followed closely by older adults and young adults.

Geographically, certain regions such as West Virginia have reported the highest rates of overdose deaths, with an age-adjusted rate of 80.9 per 100,000 people in 2022. The crisis is further complicated by the emergence of polysubstance use, where fentanyl is often combined with other drugs, making overdose events even more likely. Addressing this issue requires urgent public health interventions and community-based strategies to prevent further loss of life.

For more detailed statistics and insights into the current overdose crisis, you can visit sources like the Centers for Disease Control and Prevention or the Addiction Group.

The impact of drug overdoses on families and communities is profound, weaving a complex tapestry of grief, trauma, and disruption that often goes unrecognized. As overdose rates continue to soar, so too do the personal stories behind each statistic. Families are left shattered, grappling with the immediate and long-term consequences of losing a loved one to addiction. For these families, the emotional toll can be overwhelming. Grieving parents, spouses, and children often navigate feelings of guilt, anger, and confusion. The sudden absence of a family member alters day-to-day life, disrupting routines and destabilizing relationships. Children may face not only the loss of a parent but also the challenge of living in environments marked by instability and uncertainty.

Financial strain is another significant consequence of overdose deaths. The loss of a primary income earner can thrust families into precarious situations, often forcing them to make difficult choices about housing, education, and healthcare. According to the National Institute on Drug Abuse, families may face increased medical bills, funeral expenses, and the costs associated with treatment for surviving family members who may be struggling with addiction themselves. These economic hardships compound the emotional distress, creating a vicious cycle that can further entrench families in poverty and despair.

The ripple effects of overdoses extend beyond the immediate family unit. In communities experiencing high rates of overdose, the collective grief can manifest in various ways. Local healthcare systems, often already stretched thin, find themselves overwhelmed as they respond to an influx of overdose cases. Emergency rooms may become battlegrounds for saving lives, leaving healthcare providers grappling with burnout and the emotional toll of repeated tragedies. A study published in JAMA Network Open noted that communities with higher rates of overdoses experience significant strain on public health resources, leading to longer wait times for treatment and decreased quality of care for all patients.

Schools, too, bear the burden of this crisis. Students who have lost family members to overdoses may struggle with grief, anxiety, and depression. They often require additional support to navigate their feelings, yet schools may lack the resources to provide adequate mental health services. Teachers and counselors may feel ill-equipped to address the unique challenges faced by these students, resulting in a cycle of neglect that can hinder educational outcomes. The Centers for Disease Control and Prevention (CDC) emphasizes the importance of supportive environments in schools to help children process their grief and promote resilience.

The social fabric of communities frays as the stigma surrounding addiction and overdose persists. Many families feel isolated, ashamed, and unable to speak openly about their struggles. This silence can prevent individuals from seeking the help they need, further entrenching them in a cycle of addiction and despair. A survey by the Substance Abuse and Mental Health Services Administration (SAMHSA) found that stigma remains a significant barrier to seeking treatment, with many individuals fearing judgment from peers and family. Community awareness and education initiatives can play a crucial role in combating this stigma, fostering a culture of understanding and support.

Efforts to address the overdose crisis must consider the profound impact on families and communities. Comprehensive support systems that provide not only grief counseling but also practical assistance are essential. Families affected by overdose require access to resources that can help them navigate their new reality. This may include financial counseling, mental health services, and connections to support groups where they can share their experiences with others facing similar challenges. Research indicates that peer support groups can be instrumental in helping families cope with their losses and find pathways to healing.

Community organizations and initiatives focused on prevention, education, and recovery are vital in mitigating the far-reaching effects of the overdose crisis. Public health campaigns that promote awareness of the risks associated with drug use can empower individuals to make informed choices and seek help when needed. The CDC recommends community-based approaches that incorporate local voices and resources to effectively address the unique needs of each community . These efforts can help rebuild trust and safety within neighborhoods impacted by the overdose epidemic.

As families and communities confront the aftermath of drug overdoses, they face an urgent need for collective action. Addressing the overdose crisis requires a multifaceted approach that prioritizes the needs of those directly affected. Community leaders, healthcare providers, and policymakers must collaborate to create supportive environments where individuals can access treatment and families can find solace in shared experiences.

The pain of losing a loved one to an overdose is immeasurable, yet there is hope in the resilience of families and communities. By fostering a sense of connection and understanding, it is possible to begin healing the wounds inflicted by this crisis. With a commitment to addressing stigma and providing comprehensive support, communities can reclaim their strength and work toward a future free from the devastating impacts of addiction and overdose. In recognizing the humanity behind each statistic, we can transform grief into action, creating pathways for recovery, hope, and renewal.

The overdose crisis in the United States has sparked a series of responses from government and community organizations, driven by the urgent need to address the escalating number of deaths and the devastating impact on families and neighborhoods. As the opioid epidemic continues to evolve, the strategies implemented to combat it have also adapted, revealing both successes and ongoing challenges.

Government interventions began to gain momentum as opioid-related fatalities reached alarming levels. The Centers for Disease Control and Prevention (CDC) issued guidelines aimed at curbing opioid prescriptions, emphasizing the necessity for healthcare providers to explore alternative pain management solutions. This initiative seeks to reduce over-prescription practices, which have been pivotal in fueling the epidemic. Additionally, federal and state governments have allocated substantial funding to combat the crisis. The Substance Abuse and Mental Health Services Administration (SAMHSA) has distributed grants to enhance treatment options and recovery services at local levels.

Despite these efforts, many advocates argue that the funding provided is insufficient when weighed against the crisis's scale. According to the National Institute on Drug Abuse (NIDA), opioid overdoses accounted for over 80,000 deaths in 2021 alone, highlighting the urgent need for resources that match the epidemic's enormity. While billions of dollars have been dedicated to addressing the opioid crisis, critics emphasize that the allocation often lacks equitable distribution, particularly in rural areas where access to treatment and recovery resources is limited.

Community organizations have emerged as vital contributors to the response to the overdose crisis. Local initiatives focus on delivering essential support and education to those affected by addiction. Harm reduction strategies have gained traction, prioritizing the health and safety of individuals who use drugs. These programs include needle exchange services and the distribution of naloxone, a medication capable of reversing opioid overdoses. The National Harm Reduction Coalition has played a significant role in advocating for such strategies, which are crucial in reducing the stigma surrounding addiction while saving lives.

While harm reduction approaches can be contentious, they represent a necessary shift in addressing addiction. Critics express concern that these measures might enable substance use instead of promoting recovery; however, evidence shows that harm reduction can significantly reduce overdose fatalities and other health risks associated with drug use. The focus on saving lives has become paramount as the overdose crisis continues to claim lives at an alarming rate.

Law enforcement's role in the overdose crisis response has also evolved. Many police departments are implementing programs designed to redirect individuals struggling with addiction toward treatment instead of arrest. Initiatives like Law Enforcement Assisted Diversion (LEAD) empower officers to refer individuals to community-based treatment options. This progressive shift in policing practices can significantly influence how addiction is treated within the justice system. However, the effectiveness of these programs often hinges on the availability of funding for treatment services and comprehensive community support.

Recognizing the social determinants of health has become increasingly important in addressing substance use and overdose. Factors such as poverty, lack of access to healthcare, and systemic inequalities significantly contribute to addiction rates and overdose fatalities. Community organizations that provide comprehensive support services—ranging from housing assistance to mental health resources—are crucial in creating sustainable solutions for individuals grappling with addiction. Programs that integrate these services have shown promise in reducing overdose rates and fostering long-term recovery.

Public awareness campaigns play a pivotal role in shaping perceptions surrounding the overdose crisis. Initiatives aimed at educating the public about the dangers of drug use, particularly regarding fentanyl-laced substances, help shift public understanding and reduce stigma. Campaigns like "Reach Out" and "Stop Overdose" utilize social media platforms and community outreach to disseminate critical information, fostering a more informed public.

Despite the various initiatives being implemented, the overdose crisis continues to evolve. The increasing prevalence of synthetic opioids, particularly fentanyl, presents new challenges for prevention and treatment efforts. Policymakers and community leaders must remain vigilant and adaptable in their approaches to meet the changing landscape of drug use and overdose. Continuous evaluation of strategies is vital to ensure that responses are effective and relevant.

The collective efforts of government agencies, community organizations, and law enforcement illustrate a commitment to addressing the overdose crisis. While progress is evident, the ongoing challenges highlight the necessity for cohesive and sustained responses. Collaboration among these entities is essential to creating a comprehensive framework that prioritizes public health, reduces stigma, and ultimately saves lives.

Overall, the response to the overdose crisis must evolve continually, considering emerging trends and the broader context of substance use. Efforts that incorporate harm reduction, equitable funding, community support, and public education will be pivotal in combatting the epidemic. By fostering collaboration and understanding the complexities of addiction, communities can create a more supportive environment for those affected, paving the way for healing and recovery.

Government agencies, local communities, and law enforcement are all actively responding to the overdose crisis with diverse strategies. Despite measures to limit prescriptions, expand treatment access, and improve harm reduction, synthetic opioids like fentanyl present new dangers that call for adaptable, urgent approaches. By emphasizing harm reduction and education, community programs address both the immediate safety of users and the need to reduce stigma, while policing programs aim to shift focus from criminalization to support. As this crisis persists, these efforts reveal the complexities of addiction and underscore the need for continued collaboration and targeted funding to save lives and promote recovery across all communities.

Crime and Drug-Related Criminal Behavior

The relationship between drugs and crime is a complex and multifaceted issue, rooted in a mix of desperation, economics, and survival instincts. Communities across the United States face rising crime rates that often correlate directly with drug trafficking, addiction, and the constant demand for illegal substances. Cartels and criminal organizations fuel these cycles of violence and dependency, but the ripple effects go beyond organized crime. Street-level dealers, users, and everyday citizens become intertwined in the drug economy, leading to theft, violence, and tragic loss.

Each step along the supply chain — from production and trafficking to local sales and use — leaves a trail of criminal activity that impacts communities and perpetuates cycles of fear and instability. Law enforcement agencies, while working to dismantle major trafficking networks, also contend with the local, day-to-day crimes that addiction fuels. Whether through robbery, assault, or more organized crime rings, the impact of drugs on crime challenges both the legal system and social services. As this chapter delves deeper, it unravels the intersections between drug-related criminal behavior, trafficking networks, and the social and economic tolls they exact on individuals and communities alike.

The connection between drug use and criminal behavior is complex and multidimensional, deeply intertwined with addiction's economic, social, and psychological impacts. It fuels cycles of theft, violence, and trafficking, creating lasting effects within communities.

Addiction is a significant driver of property crimes, as individuals struggling with substance dependence often turn to theft to support their habits. This pattern is common among users of expensive substances like heroin, cocaine, and opioids. With drugs being both addictive and costly, users often deplete their own resources quickly, leading them to commit crimes to obtain cash or valuable items to sell. These crimes include shoplifting, burglary, vehicle theft, and pickpocketing. Because the primary motive is often immediate financial gain, users may disregard the consequences and risks associated with getting caught. Over time, theft becomes more frequent, not only harming the victims directly affected but also damaging the broader community's sense of safety.

The addictive nature of certain drugs, particularly stimulants and opioids, exacerbates these patterns. Opioids like heroin and synthetic opioids such as fentanyl cause rapid physical dependence, leading to withdrawal symptoms that drive users to seek relief at any cost. Stimulants like methamphetamine and crack cocaine, though not inducing the same physical withdrawal, create intense psychological cravings, contributing to desperation that can result in theft or robbery. The sheer need to stave off withdrawal or fulfill intense cravings can make individuals feel trapped in a cycle that compels them to commit crimes, regardless of their background or prior criminal history.

Violence is another significant facet of the relationship between drug use and crime. The illegal drug market is characterized by an absence of legal regulation, making it prone to violent conflicts. Users themselves may become violent due to the psychological effects of certain substances. Stimulants, including cocaine and methamphetamine, can induce paranoia, hallucinations, and aggression. Under the influence of these drugs, individuals may act out in violent ways, posing risks not only to themselves but also to those around them. In some cases, these incidents involve harm to family members, friends, or even strangers, as users react unpredictably to the substances in their system.

Beyond individual users, violence is deeply embedded in the trafficking networks that sustain the illegal drug trade. Cartels and organized crime groups rely on a combination of force, intimidation, and violence to protect their operations. To maintain control over production and distribution routes, these groups engage in ruthless tactics, including assassinations, kidnappings, and armed confrontations. In Mexico, for example, drug cartels frequently employ violence to assert control over territory, with consequences that often spill over the border into the United States. Cities and towns that lie along these trafficking routes are especially vulnerable to the effects of cartel-related violence.

In urban areas within the United States, gang-related violence often overlaps with the drug trade. Many street gangs control local drug distribution, particularly in lower-income neighborhoods, where they compete for dominance and territory. Conflicts between rival gangs frequently escalate into gun violence, affecting innocent bystanders and contributing to elevated homicide rates in these communities. Gang members also use violence as a means of controlling those within their ranks, pressuring younger or lower-level members into committing crimes on behalf of the organization. This approach ensures loyalty and minimizes the risk of betrayal but also traps individuals in cycles of violence and criminality.

Trafficking itself represents a major criminal enterprise, with complex supply chains that cross international borders and involve numerous actors at various levels. At the top are powerful cartels and criminal organizations that oversee the production and transportation of large quantities of drugs. These organizations employ a sophisticated network of traffickers, distributors, and street-level dealers, each playing a role in ensuring the drugs reach their intended market. Cartels use a variety of smuggling techniques, including concealed compartments in vehicles, tunnels, and even drones, to evade law enforcement and transport drugs into the United States. Once inside the country, drugs are distributed through networks that extend into cities, suburbs, and rural areas alike.

The involvement of organized crime in drug trafficking has far-reaching implications, as these organizations often diversify their criminal activities. Many cartels not only smuggle drugs but also engage in human trafficking, arms smuggling, and money laundering. By diversifying their operations, they increase their resilience to law enforcement crackdowns on any single activity. This diversification also strengthens their financial base, allowing them to exert influence over corrupt officials and law enforcement agents. In some cases, cartel influence infiltrates the political structures of the regions where they operate, creating environments where violence and corruption are deeply entrenched.

At the community level, drug trafficking generates crime and insecurity, impacting daily life in affected areas. Street-level trafficking brings with it violence as competing dealers fight for control over valuable turf. Families in these areas experience heightened fear, knowing that their streets are no longer safe as trafficking brings gun violence, robberies, and assaults close to home. The presence of dealers in residential neighborhoods creates an atmosphere where community trust erodes, and ordinary residents feel vulnerable. The illicit economy surrounding drug trafficking undermines the local legitimate economy, as law-abiding businesses struggle to operate amidst the risk of violence or pressure from organized crime networks.

In response, communities often become polarized. Some members push for increased policing and harsher penalties, believing that a strong law enforcement presence can curb the spread of drugs and violence. Others, however, advocate for community-based interventions that emphasize addiction treatment and support for those vulnerable to becoming involved in trafficking. These advocates argue that poverty, lack of opportunity, and social isolation drive individuals into the drug trade, and that addressing these issues at the root is crucial for lasting change.

Meanwhile, trafficking-related crime perpetuates cycles of trauma within these communities. Children growing up in areas impacted by high trafficking rates witness violence, experience the destabilizing effects of addiction within families, and are often left without stable support systems as family members become entangled in the criminal justice system. Schools, healthcare providers, and social services become overwhelmed as they attempt to address the complex needs arising from these environments, struggling to offer adequate support with limited resources.

The impact of the drug trade's intersection with crime thus extends far beyond the immediate individuals involved. It radiates through communities, destabilizing families, perpetuating fear, and demanding responses that are often reactive rather than proactive. The result is a costly cycle that drains resources, traumatizes individuals, and strains the social fabric of neighborhoods across the country, underlining the urgent need for systemic responses that prioritize prevention, rehabilitation, and community healing.

At the community level, drug trafficking generates crime and insecurity, significantly impacting daily life. As street-level drug operations proliferate, violence often erupts between competing dealers, who clash for dominance over lucrative territories. This persistent conflict instills fear in local residents, who must navigate streets rife with the threat of gun violence, robberies, and assaults. The resulting atmosphere of intimidation erodes trust within neighborhoods, where families once felt secure.

The presence of drug dealers and trafficking activities not only alters the immediate landscape but also undermines the local economy. Legitimate businesses struggle to survive in environments overshadowed by crime and the constant threat of violence, deterring customers and investments. As the illicit drug trade flourishes, community resources become strained. Law enforcement agencies are tasked with increased policing efforts, diverting attention from other pressing community needs, such as education and social services.

Trauma becomes a common thread in these communities, particularly for children who grow up amidst the violence and instability. Witnessing drug-related crime can lead to lasting psychological effects, and the absence of stable role models may push young individuals toward involvement in the drug trade or criminal activity.

Efforts to address these issues often result in polarized community responses. Some advocate for stricter law enforcement and punitive measures, believing that increased police presence can deter drug-related crime. Others argue for a focus on harm reduction and community support, highlighting that addressing the root causes of addiction and providing access to resources can be more effective in the long term.

Community members frequently find themselves at a crossroads, torn between the desire for safety and the need for compassion. Schools, healthcare providers, and social services are inundated with the consequences of drug trafficking, grappling with how best to support those affected while also trying to foster a sense of hope and stability.

The pervasive nature of drug-related crime creates a cycle that drains community resources and exacerbates social divisions. Areas plagued by trafficking face diminished quality of life, as residents grapple with fear, instability, and the profound effects of addiction on families and social structures. Ultimately, the challenge lies in fostering resilience within communities while addressing the systemic issues that fuel the drug trade and its associated criminal behaviors.

The Social Cost: Impact on Communities and Families

The social cost of drug addiction extends far beyond the individual; it ripples through families, communities, and society at large. As the opioid crisis and other substance use disorders continue to escalate, the devastating impact on those caught in the cycle of addiction becomes increasingly evident. Families experience profound emotional, financial, and psychological strain as they navigate the challenges of supporting a loved one battling addiction. Parents may find themselves torn between offering help and protecting their children from the associated dangers, often leading to conflict and emotional distance.

Communities bear the brunt of these social costs as well. Drug addiction fuels crime rates, exacerbates poverty, and places immense pressure on local services such as healthcare, law enforcement, and education. Public resources become stretched as communities struggle to provide adequate support for those affected, often resulting in a reactive rather than proactive approach to dealing with addiction and its consequences.

The social fabric of neighborhoods frays as trust erodes, leading to increased isolation among residents. Children growing up in these environments may face disrupted family structures, lack of role models, and limited access to education and recreational opportunities. The cycle of addiction and its repercussions create a landscape where hope is overshadowed by despair, highlighting the urgent need for comprehensive solutions that address not only the symptoms of addiction but also its root causes. This chapter delves into the multifaceted social costs of drug addiction, exploring how they shape the lives of individuals and the fabric of communities.

Drug addiction and the associated crime significantly impact families and communities, creating a cycle of distress that can be challenging to escape. Families often bear the brunt of the emotional, psychological, and financial turmoil resulting from a loved one's substance use disorder. Relationships within families can become strained, as trust erodes and communication breaks down. Parents may feel overwhelmed by their inability to help their children, leading to feelings of guilt, anger, and helplessness. Siblings may feel neglected as attention is diverted to the addicted family member, resulting in a sense of isolation and resentment.

The financial strain on families can be devastating. The costs associated with addiction, including treatment expenses, legal fees, and lost income due to job instability or absenteeism, can lead to significant economic hardship. Families may find themselves in a precarious situation, forced to make difficult decisions about budgeting for essential needs like housing and food while trying to support the addiction or seek treatment. Many families may also face the loss of their primary breadwinner, either due to incarceration or death, further exacerbating financial difficulties.

Communities experience similar repercussions. The prevalence of drug addiction leads to increased crime rates, including theft, violence, and drug trafficking, creating an environment of fear and insecurity. Residents may feel unsafe in their neighborhoods, leading to decreased community engagement and social cohesion. As crime rates rise, so does the demand for law enforcement, which can strain public resources and create a reactive approach to dealing with addiction and crime rather than addressing underlying issues.

Schools and educational institutions bear the brunt of these social costs as well. Children from families affected by drug addiction may struggle academically due to instability at home, lack of support, or emotional distress. This can result in higher dropout rates and a lower likelihood of pursuing higher education, perpetuating a cycle of poverty and limited opportunity. Teachers and school administrators often find themselves on the front lines, dealing with the effects of addiction in their students' lives.

The stigma associated with drug addiction further complicates these dynamics. Families affected by addiction may feel isolated and judged by their communities, preventing them from seeking help or accessing necessary resources. This stigma can create barriers to treatment, as individuals may be reluctant to admit they have a problem or seek help due to fear of judgment. Communities, too, can become divided in their responses to addiction, with some advocating for harsher penalties and others pushing for compassion and support.

The mental health of both individuals struggling with addiction and their families often deteriorates in this environment. Anxiety, depression, and other mental health disorders can become more prevalent as families navigate the challenges of addiction. The ongoing stress and trauma can lead to a cycle of mental health issues that further complicate recovery efforts. Access to mental health resources is crucial, yet often limited in communities heavily impacted by drug addiction.

Addressing the multifaceted impact of drug addiction requires a comprehensive approach. Families need access to support systems that offer guidance, education, and resources to help them navigate the complexities of addiction. Community programs that focus on prevention, education, and rehabilitation can foster resilience and provide individuals with the tools necessary to break the cycle of addiction. Collaborative efforts between local organizations, schools, and healthcare providers can help create a supportive environment for individuals and families affected by addiction.

Investing in community-based solutions can lead to healthier, more resilient neighborhoods. Programs that focus on youth engagement, education, and mental health support can help mitigate the impacts of addiction on future generations. Encouraging open dialogue about addiction can help reduce stigma and promote understanding, creating a more supportive community environment.

The impacts of drug addiction and crime extend far beyond the individual, creating a ripple effect that affects families and communities. Acknowledging these challenges is the first step toward fostering resilience and creating solutions that can help break the cycle of addiction and its consequences. By prioritizing support for families and communities, we can work toward a healthier future for all.

The long-term effects of drug addiction on children, schools, and neighborhoods are profound and multifaceted, creating challenges that can persist across generations. Children who grow up in environments where drug addiction is prevalent face significant hurdles in their emotional, social, and educational development.

Children in homes affected by substance use disorders often experience neglect, inconsistent parenting, and a lack of stable support systems. This instability can lead to various psychological issues, including anxiety, depression, and behavioral problems. A study published in Child Development found that children in these environments are more likely to develop attachment issues, which can hinder their ability to form healthy relationships later in life. The absence of a nurturing environment can also lead to difficulties in emotional regulation, increasing the risk of substance use in their adolescent and adult years.

Educationally, the impact of drug addiction on children can be equally devastating. Research indicates that children from families struggling with addiction often have lower academic achievement and higher rates of school dropout. Factors contributing to this trend include frequent absences due to family instability, lack of parental support for education, and the emotional toll of living in a high-stress environment. A report from the National Institute on Drug Abuse highlights that children of parents with substance use disorders are at a higher risk of being involved in the juvenile justice system, often due to behavioral issues stemming from their home life.

Schools are on the front lines of these challenges. Educators may encounter students who display signs of trauma, difficulty concentrating, or behavioral problems, all of which can stem from their home environment. Schools that lack adequate resources to address these issues may struggle to support affected students, leading to a cycle of underachievement and disengagement. Programs designed to provide social-emotional support and resources for at-risk students can help mitigate some of these effects, yet many schools are underfunded and unable to meet the growing demand for such services.

Neighborhoods impacted by drug addiction also bear the consequences of these issues. High rates of drug-related crime contribute to an environment of fear and instability. As crime rates increase, community cohesion often deteriorates, leading to isolation among residents. This breakdown can hinder community efforts to address addiction and its associated challenges. Studies show that neighborhoods with high levels of drug activity tend to have lower property values and reduced investment in local services, creating a cycle of decline that can be difficult to reverse.

The long-term effects on neighborhoods can extend to public health. Communities with prevalent drug issues often see increased rates of infectious diseases, mental health disorders, and other public health crises. Access to healthcare may become limited as local services are strained under the pressure of increased demand. This can result in a lack of preventive care and support for families affected by addiction, perpetuating the cycle of disadvantage.

Addressing the long-term effects of drug addiction requires a comprehensive and community-focused approach. Initiatives that provide support for families, such as parenting programs, substance use treatment, and mental health services, can create a foundation for recovery. Schools must be equipped with the resources to offer trauma-informed care, allowing educators to identify and support students in need effectively.

Community engagement is essential to rebuilding neighborhoods affected by drug addiction. Initiatives that foster social cohesion, such as community events, support groups, and educational programs, can help to restore trust and collaboration among residents. Local organizations can play a vital role in providing resources and support, helping to create a network of care that benefits families and children.

As society grapples with the widespread impact of drug addiction, recognizing and addressing the long-term effects on children, schools, and neighborhoods is crucial. By focusing on prevention, support, and community resilience, we can work toward breaking the cycle of addiction and its consequences, ultimately fostering healthier environments for future generations.

The opioid crisis has profoundly affected many communities across the United States, leaving lasting scars on families, neighborhoods, and local economies. Below are examples of several communities particularly impacted by the crisis, illustrating the varying degrees and forms of its influence.

1. Huntington, West Virginia

Huntington, West Virginia, has often been described as the epicenter of the opioid epidemic in the United States. The city has one of the highest rates of overdose deaths in the country, largely driven by prescription opioids, heroin, and fentanyl. Factors contributing to this crisis include economic decline, limited access to healthcare, and a lack of job opportunities, which have left many residents vulnerable to addiction.

In response to the crisis, local leaders have implemented harm reduction strategies, including needle exchange programs and increased access to treatment facilities. The city has also seen community organizations step in to provide support and education about the dangers of drug use. Despite these efforts, the community continues to struggle with high overdose rates, showcasing the persistent impact of addiction on daily life.

2. Philadelphia, Pennsylvania

Philadelphia has faced significant challenges due to the opioid crisis, with an alarming increase in overdose deaths in recent years. The city's Kensington neighborhood, in particular, has become notorious for its open drug use and rampant addiction. Social services in the area have been overwhelmed, as many residents battle substance use disorders without adequate support.

The city has implemented several initiatives to combat the crisis, including supervised injection sites and increased funding for addiction treatment programs. Community organizations have mobilized to provide outreach services, but the scale of the problem remains daunting. Philadelphia's experience highlights how urban environments can amplify the effects of addiction, leading to public health and safety concerns.

3. Akron, Ohio

In Akron, Ohio, the opioid epidemic has dramatically affected the community, with rising overdose deaths attributed primarily to fentanyl-laced drugs. The city has witnessed the devastation of families and neighborhoods, as addiction often leads to increased crime and social instability.

Local leaders have taken steps to address the crisis by expanding access to treatment and recovery services. Community-driven initiatives, such as peer support programs, aim to engage those struggling with addiction and promote recovery. However, the lasting effects of the crisis continue to create barriers to healing and recovery within the community.

4. New Hampshire

New Hampshire has one of the highest rates of opioid overdose deaths in the nation, with rural areas often facing unique challenges. The state has struggled to combat addiction due to limited access to treatment facilities and a lack of public transportation, which hinders residents from seeking help.

The opioid crisis has also strained law enforcement and public health resources, leading to a concerted effort by state officials to implement comprehensive strategies. New Hampshire has invested in prevention and education programs, as well as expanded access to naloxone, a life-saving drug that reverses opioid overdoses. Despite these efforts, the stigma surrounding addiction remains a significant barrier to recovery for many residents.

5. Camden, New Jersey

Camden has been grappling with the opioid crisis, experiencing high rates of drug-related deaths and significant challenges related to public safety and health. The city's socioeconomic struggles, including poverty and unemployment, have exacerbated the crisis, making residents more susceptible to addiction.

Community organizations in Camden have focused on outreach and education, striving to create a supportive environment for individuals battling addiction. Local leaders have also sought to increase access to treatment and prevention programs, but the ongoing violence and crime related to drug trafficking complicate these efforts.

6. Baltimore, Maryland

Baltimore has experienced a surge in opioid-related overdoses, with the city often ranking among the highest in the nation for overdose deaths. The crisis has disproportionately affected marginalized communities, where a lack of resources and healthcare access has contributed to higher rates of addiction.

In response to the epidemic, Baltimore has implemented harm reduction strategies, such as safe consumption sites and expanded treatment options. Community organizations work tirelessly to engage those affected by addiction, providing support and resources. However, the ongoing stigma and fear associated with addiction continue to challenge recovery efforts.

7. rural America

The opioid crisis has also significantly impacted rural communities across the United States, where limited access to healthcare and social services makes it difficult for residents to receive treatment. In many cases, the stigma surrounding addiction prevents individuals from seeking help, further entrenching the crisis.

For instance, towns in rural Kentucky and West Virginia have reported alarming increases in overdose deaths, primarily linked to prescription opioids and heroin. The lack of employment opportunities and economic decline in these areas has contributed to the prevalence of addiction, leading to calls for greater investment in treatment and prevention programs tailored to the unique needs of rural populations.

8. The Native American Communities

Native American communities have faced disproportionate impacts from the opioid crisis, exacerbating existing health disparities and socioeconomic challenges. High rates of substance use disorders, coupled with limited access to healthcare services, have created a public health emergency in many tribes across the country.

Efforts to address the crisis in Native American communities include culturally appropriate treatment programs and collaborations with tribal leadership to develop effective prevention strategies. The response has emphasized the importance of addressing historical trauma and building trust within communities to promote healing and recovery.

9. St. Louis, Missouri

St. Louis has faced a severe opioid crisis that has left a profound impact on the community and its residents. The city has experienced a dramatic rise in overdose deaths, particularly related to heroin and synthetic opioids like fentanyl. In recent years, St. Louis has consistently ranked among the cities with the highest rates of drug overdose fatalities in the United States.

Factors contributing to the crisis include economic decline, high poverty rates, and limited access to healthcare and addiction treatment services. The city's struggles with crime and violence are often exacerbated by the prevalence of drug trafficking, creating an environment where addiction flourishes. Many residents find themselves caught in a cycle of substance use that impacts not only their health but also their families and communities.

In response to the crisis, local leaders have implemented various initiatives aimed at harm reduction and treatment access. Efforts include the distribution of naloxone, a medication that reverses opioid overdoses, and the establishment of syringe exchange programs to reduce the spread of infectious diseases. Community organizations have mobilized to provide support services and promote awareness about the dangers of drug use. Despite these efforts, the high rates of overdose deaths and the stigma surrounding addiction present ongoing challenges for St. Louis.

The city's experience highlights the need for a comprehensive and coordinated response to the opioid epidemic, emphasizing prevention, treatment, and support for individuals and families affected by addiction. The crisis in St. Louis serves as a stark reminder of the urgent need for sustained efforts to address the complex factors contributing to the opioid epidemic and its far-reaching effects on communities.

These examples illustrate the widespread and diverse impact of the opioid crisis on communities throughout the United States. Each community faces unique challenges and responses, but the common thread remains the urgent need for comprehensive strategies to address addiction, support recovery, and foster healthier environments for all residents. The long-term consequences of this crisis extend beyond individuals to affect families, neighborhoods, and the fabric of society as a whole.

To find statistics and understand the effects of the drug crisis in specific areas, researchers can access various resources. Local health departments often publish annual reports detailing overdose rates, drug-related fatalities, and community health assessments. The Centers for Disease Control and Prevention (CDC) provides national data on drug overdoses, which can be broken down by state and local jurisdictions. The National Institute on Drug Abuse (NIDA) offers insights into trends in substance use and addiction, including demographic breakdowns. Additionally, local newspapers and media outlets frequently cover the impacts of drug use on communities, highlighting personal stories and expert opinions.

Community organizations and non-profits, such as the National Council on Alcoholism and Drug Dependence (NCADD), can also provide localized data and impact assessments. They often conduct surveys and publish findings that reflect the state of addiction and its consequences in specific neighborhoods. Engaging with these resources will yield a comprehensive picture of how the drug crisis affects different communities.

For a more detailed understanding, you can explore sources such as:
- CDC Drug Overdose Data
- NIDA Statistics
- Local health department websites or reports.

Recovery, Rehabilitation, and Treatment

Recovery, rehabilitation, and treatment stand at the forefront of the battle against addiction, serving as essential pathways for individuals seeking to reclaim their lives from substance use disorders. The journey to recovery is often intricate and deeply personal, requiring a multifaceted approach that encompasses medical, psychological, and social support. Successful rehabilitation not only addresses the physical dependence on drugs or alcohol but also the underlying psychological issues that may have contributed to the addiction.

Effective treatment programs employ a variety of methods, including detoxification, individual and group therapy, medication-assisted treatment (MAT), and ongoing aftercare support. Evidence suggests that integrating behavioral therapies with medical interventions can significantly improve outcomes for individuals in recovery. Additionally, a strong support network, including family involvement and peer support groups, plays a crucial role in sustaining recovery and preventing relapse.

As awareness of the addiction crisis grows, communities are increasingly focusing on expanding access to effective treatment options and creating supportive environments that foster recovery. This chapter will explore various treatment modalities, highlighting successful approaches and innovative practices that emphasize holistic healing. It will also examine the importance of community engagement and policy initiatives aimed at enhancing treatment accessibility, ultimately promoting a culture of recovery that empowers individuals and strengthens families and communities.

The landscape of drug addiction treatment is multifaceted, incorporating various strategies designed to meet the unique needs of individuals grappling with substance use disorders. This comprehensive approach recognizes that addiction is not merely a physical ailment but a complex interplay of psychological, social, and environmental factors. Consequently, effective treatment requires a combination of methods tailored to address these diverse elements.

Detoxification, or detox, is often the first step in the recovery journey. This process involves the safe removal of drugs from the body while managing withdrawal symptoms. Depending on the substance used, withdrawal can range from uncomfortable to life-threatening, necessitating medical supervision. Detox typically occurs in specialized facilities where healthcare professionals monitor patients' health and comfort. The length of detox varies based on several factors, including the substance used, the duration of use, and the individual's overall health. For example, opioid withdrawal can last several days and may involve significant physical and psychological symptoms, making medical oversight essential.

Following detox, individuals usually enter a rehabilitation program. Rehabilitation can take place in various settings, including residential or outpatient facilities. Residential rehab offers a structured environment where individuals can immerse themselves in recovery without the distractions of daily life. Programs generally last anywhere from 30 to 90 days, providing intensive therapy and support. These programs often include a range of therapeutic modalities tailored to individual needs, including cognitive-behavioral therapy (CBT), which focuses on identifying and changing negative thought patterns, and dialectical behavior therapy (DBT), which emphasizes emotional regulation and interpersonal effectiveness.

Outpatient rehab is another viable option for many individuals. This approach allows them to live at home while attending scheduled treatment sessions. Outpatient programs provide flexibility for those who need to maintain work or family obligations but still require structured support. These programs can vary in intensity, with some offering daily therapy sessions and others providing weekly support groups. Regardless of the format, effective outpatient treatment often includes a combination of group and individual therapy, ensuring that individuals receive the support they need.

Counseling plays a pivotal role in the recovery process, addressing the psychological aspects of addiction. Individual counseling provides a safe space for individuals to explore their feelings, motivations, and triggers. This one-on-one interaction fosters a strong therapeutic alliance, which can be vital for effective treatment. Additionally, group counseling offers an opportunity for individuals to connect with peers facing similar challenges, promoting a sense of community and shared understanding. This collective experience can be incredibly empowering, as participants share their struggles and successes, learning from one another in the process.

Family counseling is another critical component of addiction treatment. Substance use disorders often disrupt family dynamics, leading to tension and conflict. Involving family members in the treatment process helps to address these issues, fostering communication and rebuilding trust. Family therapy can provide insights into the impact of addiction on relationships, allowing families to develop healthier patterns of interaction. This holistic approach ensures that all aspects of an individual's life are considered in the treatment process.

Medication-assisted treatment (MAT) has emerged as a vital strategy for addressing substance use disorders, particularly those involving opioids and alcohol. MAT combines behavioral therapy with medications to manage cravings and withdrawal symptoms, facilitating a smoother recovery process. For opioid addiction, medications such as methadone and buprenorphine work by activating the same receptors in the brain as opioids but without the same euphoric effects, helping individuals stabilize their lives while they engage in counseling and support groups. Naltrexone, another medication used in MAT, blocks the effects of opioids, reducing cravings and the risk of relapse.

In the context of alcohol addiction, MAT may involve medications such as disulfiram, which discourages drinking by causing unpleasant reactions when alcohol is consumed, or acamprosate, which helps reduce cravings. These medications can significantly improve outcomes for individuals seeking recovery, as they address the biological aspects of addiction while allowing for concurrent therapeutic interventions.

An innovative approach gaining traction is Moral Reconation Therapy (MRT), which targets the moral and ethical development of individuals in recovery. MRT is particularly beneficial for those whose substance use has led to criminal behavior or significant interpersonal conflicts. This therapy encourages participants to reflect on their values and actions, fostering accountability and encouraging ethical decision-making. Through structured sessions, individuals learn to recognize the impact of their choices on themselves and others, ultimately developing a stronger sense of social responsibility.

MRT's integration into treatment programs complements traditional counseling methods, providing individuals with essential tools to make healthier decisions and rebuild their lives post-addiction. This therapeutic approach can significantly support sustained recovery, reducing the likelihood of relapse and fostering a deeper understanding of the consequences of substance use.

Incorporating a multi-faceted approach to treatment that includes detox, rehab, counseling, medication-assisted treatment, and MRT offers individuals a comprehensive path to recovery. Each component addresses different aspects of addiction, ensuring that individuals are supported physically, emotionally, and socially throughout their healing journey. This integrated treatment approach is essential for promoting lasting recovery and improving overall quality of life for those affected by substance use disorders.

Access to effective treatment remains a significant barrier for many individuals seeking help. Stigma surrounding addiction, lack of resources, and limited availability of treatment programs contribute to the ongoing struggle for recovery. Addressing these barriers is critical for enhancing the effectiveness of treatment options and ensuring that individuals can access the support they need.

As the understanding of addiction continues to evolve, so too do the treatment options available. Research into the neurobiological underpinnings of addiction and the efficacy of various therapeutic modalities is ongoing, leading to improved strategies for addressing this complex issue. By embracing a comprehensive approach to addiction treatment that combines detox, rehabilitation, counseling, medication-assisted treatment, and innovative therapies like MRT, we can better support individuals on their journey to recovery and foster healthier communities.

The importance of continuing to refine and expand treatment options cannot be overstated. As addiction rates rise and new substances emerge, it is essential for the medical community, policymakers, and society at large to prioritize access to quality treatment. This commitment not only benefits individuals struggling with addiction but also strengthens the fabric of communities by addressing the underlying issues that contribute to substance use disorders. In doing so, we can work toward a future where recovery is not only possible but achievable for everyone.

Barriers to accessing treatment for drug addiction present significant challenges that many individuals encounter in their pursuit of recovery. Stigma surrounding addiction serves as one of the most formidable obstacles. This stigma often manifests as a societal perception that equates substance use disorders with moral failing rather than recognizing them as complex medical conditions. Individuals struggling with addiction may feel profound shame, leading to reluctance in seeking help due to fear of judgment from family, friends, and society at large. A study by Corrigan et al. (2009) highlights how internalized stigma can discourage individuals from accessing care, emphasizing the need for societal change in understanding addiction.

In addition to personal stigma, institutional stigma within healthcare settings can hinder access. Many healthcare providers lack adequate training in addiction treatment, resulting in a lack of compassion and understanding. According to the Substance Abuse and Mental Health Services Administration (SAMHSA, 2016), this gap in training often leads to substandard care for those seeking treatment. Patients may leave treatment programs feeling unheard or judged, reinforcing the stigma and discouraging future attempts to seek help. This environment contributes to the cycle of addiction and impedes recovery efforts.

The financial aspect of accessing treatment cannot be overstated. Many individuals face substantial financial barriers when seeking help for addiction, with costs associated with detoxification, rehabilitation, and counseling often being prohibitively high. According to the National Institute on Drug Abuse (NIDA, 2021), the costs of treatment can vary significantly, leaving those without adequate health insurance to navigate a complex financial landscape. Many individuals prioritize basic necessities such as housing and food over treatment, viewing it as a luxury rather than a necessity.

Insurance coverage for addiction treatment has improved in recent years due to initiatives like the Affordable Care Act, which mandates parity for mental health and substance use disorder treatment. However, numerous plans still impose high copays, deductibles, and limits on the number of covered treatment days, creating a significant financial strain. A report by the National Bureau of Economic Research (Kearney & Levine, 2015) underscores that out-of-pocket expenses remain a major barrier, with many individuals unable to afford comprehensive care, particularly when long-term treatment is essential.

Availability of treatment options is another crucial barrier. In many regions, especially rural and underserved areas, treatment facilities are scarce. The U.S. Department of Health and Human Services reports that while approximately 20 million Americans need substance use treatment, only about 10% actually receive it, primarily due to a shortage of treatment resources (HHS, 2021). This lack of availability forces individuals to travel long distances to access care, a logistical challenge that can be prohibitively expensive and time-consuming.

The disparity in treatment availability is particularly evident in rural communities, which often have fewer healthcare providers and limited access to specialized addiction treatment services. The National Rural Health Association (NRHA, 2020) emphasizes that rural residents are significantly less likely to receive adequate treatment for substance use disorders, increasing the likelihood of untreated addiction in these populations. This discrepancy not only affects individuals but also contributes to broader community health crises.

Waiting lists for treatment programs further exacerbate the problem of availability. Many individuals seeking residential rehabilitation services face long delays, forcing them to postpone care during critical moments when they may be most motivated to seek help. This delay poses a significant risk of relapse or overdose, highlighting the urgent need for expanded access to treatment resources.

Cultural factors also play a role in limiting access to treatment. In various communities, particularly marginalized ones, cultural stigma regarding addiction may discourage individuals from seeking help. Many cultures view addiction as a source of shame, creating barriers to accessing treatment and fostering isolation. Language barriers can also impede access for non-English speakers, making it challenging for them to find information about treatment options or navigate complex healthcare systems. These cultural and linguistic hurdles can alienate individuals from vital services, perpetuating cycles of addiction and poverty.

Efforts to address these barriers have gained traction in recent years. Advocacy groups and policymakers are working to combat stigma through education and awareness campaigns that aim to reshape public perceptions of addiction. Initiatives like "Know the Truth" seek to educate communities about the realities of addiction and recovery, fostering a more supportive environment for individuals seeking help.

Financial reforms are also critical in reducing barriers to treatment access. Expanded insurance coverage and increased funding for treatment programs are necessary steps in the right direction. The Mental Health Parity and Addiction Equity Act aims to ensure that mental health and substance use disorder treatments are covered on par with other medical services, making it easier for individuals to access care without overwhelming financial burdens.

Enhancing the availability of treatment options is essential for improving access. Increasing funding for community-based programs, expanding telehealth services, and incentivizing healthcare providers to practice in underserved areas can help bridge the gap in care. The COVID-19 pandemic has accelerated the adoption of telehealth in addiction treatment, demonstrating its potential to reach individuals facing barriers to in-person services.

Integrating services across various sectors can also enhance access to treatment. By creating partnerships between healthcare, social services, and community organizations, individuals can receive comprehensive support that addresses not only their substance use disorder but also related issues such as mental health, housing instability, and unemployment. This holistic approach recognizes the interconnectedness of these challenges, emphasizing the importance of addressing them in tandem.

Overcoming barriers to accessing treatment for drug addiction requires a multifaceted approach that tackles stigma, reduces costs, and increases availability. Implementing these strategies can create a more supportive environment for individuals seeking recovery, allowing them to access the help they need to reclaim their lives. As the understanding of addiction continues to evolve, it is crucial to advocate for policies and practices that prioritize access to quality treatment, paving the way for a healthier, more equitable future for all individuals impacted by substance use disorders.

Barriers to accessing treatment for drug addiction present significant challenges that many individuals encounter in their pursuit of recovery. Stigma surrounding addiction serves as one of the most formidable obstacles. This stigma often manifests as a societal perception that equates substance use disorders with moral failing rather than recognizing them as complex medical conditions. Individuals struggling with addiction may feel profound shame, leading to reluctance in seeking help due to fear of judgment from family, friends, and society at large. A study by Corrigan et al. (2009) highlights how internalized stigma can discourage individuals from accessing care, emphasizing the need for societal change in understanding addiction.

In addition to personal stigma, institutional stigma within healthcare settings can hinder access. Many healthcare providers lack adequate training in addiction treatment, resulting in a lack of compassion and understanding. According to the Substance Abuse and Mental Health Services Administration (SAMHSA, 2016), this gap in training often leads to substandard care for those seeking treatment. Patients may leave treatment programs feeling unheard or judged, reinforcing the stigma and discouraging future attempts to seek help. This environment contributes to the cycle of addiction and impedes recovery efforts.

The financial aspect of accessing treatment cannot be overstated. Many individuals face substantial financial barriers when seeking help for addiction, with costs associated with detoxification, rehabilitation, and counseling often being prohibitively high. According to the National Institute on Drug Abuse (NIDA, 2021), the costs of treatment can vary significantly, leaving those without adequate health insurance to navigate a complex financial landscape. Many individuals prioritize basic necessities such as housing and food over treatment, viewing it as a luxury rather than a necessity.

Insurance coverage for addiction treatment has improved in recent years due to initiatives like the Affordable Care Act, which mandates parity for mental health and substance use disorder treatment. However, numerous plans still impose high copays, deductibles, and limits on the number of covered treatment days, creating a significant financial strain. A report by the National Bureau of Economic Research (Kearney & Levine, 2015) underscores that out-of-pocket expenses remain a major barrier, with many individuals unable to afford comprehensive care, particularly when long-term treatment is essential.

Availability of treatment options is another crucial barrier. In many regions, especially rural and underserved areas, treatment facilities are scarce. The U.S. Department of Health and Human Services reports that while approximately 20 million Americans need substance use treatment, only about 10% actually receive it, primarily due to a shortage of treatment resources (HHS, 2021). This lack of availability forces individuals to travel long distances to access care, a logistical challenge that can be prohibitively expensive and time-consuming.

The disparity in treatment availability is particularly evident in rural communities, which often have fewer healthcare providers and limited access to specialized addiction treatment services. The National Rural Health Association (NRHA, 2020) emphasizes that rural residents are significantly less likely to receive adequate treatment for substance use disorders, increasing the likelihood of untreated addiction in these populations. This discrepancy not only affects individuals but also contributes to broader community health crises.

Waiting lists for treatment programs further exacerbate the problem of availability. Many individuals seeking residential rehabilitation services face long delays, forcing them to postpone care during critical moments when they may be most motivated to seek help. This delay poses a significant risk of relapse or overdose, highlighting the urgent need for expanded access to treatment resources.

Cultural factors also play a role in limiting access to treatment. In various communities, particularly marginalized ones, cultural stigma regarding addiction may discourage individuals from seeking help. Many cultures view addiction as a source of shame, creating barriers to accessing treatment and fostering isolation. Language barriers can also impede access for non-English speakers, making it challenging for them to find information about treatment options or navigate complex healthcare systems. These cultural and linguistic hurdles can alienate individuals from vital services, perpetuating cycles of addiction and poverty.

Efforts to address these barriers have gained traction in recent years. Advocacy groups and policymakers are working to combat stigma through education and awareness campaigns that aim to reshape public perceptions of addiction. Initiatives like "Know the Truth" seek to educate communities about the realities of addiction and recovery, fostering a more supportive environment for individuals seeking help.

Financial reforms are also critical in reducing barriers to treatment access. Expanded insurance coverage and increased funding for treatment programs are necessary steps in the right direction. The Mental Health Parity and Addiction Equity Act aims to ensure that mental health and substance use disorder treatments are covered on par with other medical services, making it easier for individuals to access care without overwhelming financial burdens.

Enhancing the availability of treatment options is essential for improving access. Increasing funding for community-based programs, expanding telehealth services, and incentivizing healthcare providers to practice in underserved areas can help bridge the gap in care. The COVID-19 pandemic has accelerated the adoption of telehealth in addiction treatment, demonstrating its potential to reach individuals facing barriers to in-person services.

Integrating services across various sectors can also enhance access to treatment. By creating partnerships between healthcare, social services, and community organizations, individuals can receive comprehensive support that addresses not only their substance use disorder but also related issues such as mental health, housing instability, and unemployment. This holistic approach recognizes the interconnectedness of these challenges, emphasizing the importance of addressing them in tandem.

Overcoming barriers to accessing treatment for drug addiction requires a multifaceted approach that tackles stigma, reduces costs, and increases availability. Implementing these strategies can create a more supportive environment for individuals seeking recovery, allowing them to access the help they need to reclaim their lives. As the understanding of addiction continues to evolve, it is crucial to advocate for policies and practices that prioritize access to quality treatment, paving the way for a healthier, more equitable future for all individuals impacted by substance use disorders.

Here are several stories of recovery and resilience that highlight the journeys individuals have taken to overcome addiction and rebuild their lives:

1. Jessica's Journey: After years of battling heroin addiction, Jessica found herself homeless and estranged from her family. She reached a breaking point after an overdose, which served as a wake-up call. Seeking help, she entered a rehabilitation program that emphasized both medical treatment and psychological support. With the assistance of therapy and support groups, she not only achieved sobriety but also began sharing her story to help others facing similar challenges.

Jessica now advocates for addiction recovery, helping others navigate the difficult path to healing.

2. Michael's Transformation: Michael struggled with alcohol addiction for over a decade, which led to the dissolution of his marriage and strained relationships with his children. Determined to change, he enrolled in a 12-step program, where he found a community of support. Through counseling, he addressed underlying issues related to his addiction and began to rebuild trust with his family. Michael now serves as a mentor for others in recovery, emphasizing the importance of resilience and the impact of community support in the recovery process.

3. Maria's Healing: Maria was a successful professional whose addiction to prescription opioids spiraled out of control, affecting her career and personal life. After hitting rock bottom, she sought treatment and discovered mindfulness and meditation as powerful tools in her recovery. Maria's journey included not just overcoming her addiction but also exploring holistic approaches to healing. She now works as a wellness coach, helping others understand the importance of mental and emotional health in addiction recovery.

4. James's Story: Growing up in a challenging environment, James turned to methamphetamine to cope with his circumstances. After several arrests and near-fatal overdoses, he decided to seek help through a local rehabilitation program that offered a combination of medication-assisted treatment and behavioral therapy. The support he received helped him develop coping strategies and life skills necessary for maintaining sobriety. James has since turned his life around, focusing on education and community service, aiming to inspire those who are still struggling.

5. Sarah's Advocacy: Sarah's battle with addiction began in her teenage years, fueled by a tumultuous home life. After experiencing multiple relapses, she found a program that focused on trauma-informed care. This approach helped her understand the root

causes of her addiction and how to cope with them. Sarah now works as an advocate for policy change in addiction treatment, highlighting the need for compassionate and comprehensive approaches to recovery.

6. David's Redemption: David was once a promising athlete who succumbed to the pressures of performance and turned to anabolic steroids to enhance his abilities. His addiction spiraled out of control, leading to health complications and estrangement from his family. After hitting rock bottom, David entered a rehabilitation program focused on physical and mental health. Through therapy, he learned to channel his energy into fitness rather than drugs. Today, David is a personal trainer and wellness advocate, using his experience to educate others about the dangers of substance abuse in sports.

7. Emily's Second Chance: Emily, a former nurse, became addicted to prescription painkillers after an accident. Her addiction led to job loss and the destruction of her relationships. After several failed attempts to quit on her own, Emily entered a holistic recovery program that combined traditional treatment with yoga and mindfulness practices. This approach not only helped her achieve sobriety but also allowed her to reconnect with her passion for nursing. Emily now works in addiction recovery, providing care and support to others struggling with similar challenges.

8. Aaron's Advocacy: Aaron faced a tumultuous upbringing, leading him to drugs as an escape. After years of battling addiction and multiple stints in rehab, he finally found a program that addressed his trauma. Inspired by his journey, Aaron became a peer recovery specialist, helping others navigate the complexities of addiction and recovery. His advocacy focuses on the importance of addressing mental health and trauma in the treatment process, emphasizing that recovery is a continuous journey that requires ongoing support.

9. Rachel's Resilience: Rachel struggled with alcohol addiction for years, impacting her career and family life. After a near-fatal overdose, she recognized the need for change and entered a rehabilitation

program focused on cognitive-behavioral therapy. Through hard work and dedication, Rachel rebuilt her life, reconnecting with her children and finding fulfillment in community service. Now a recovery coach, she helps others develop the tools and strategies necessary for lasting sobriety.

10. Tom's Transformation: Tom's addiction to opioids began after a legitimate prescription for pain management. What started as a medical necessity turned into a life-altering addiction. After losing his job and nearly losing his family, Tom sought help through a medication-assisted treatment program. He learned to navigate his cravings and developed healthier coping mechanisms. Tom now shares his story through public speaking engagements, raising awareness about the complexities of prescription drug addiction and the importance of seeking help.

These stories exemplify the strength and determination individuals can harness to overcome addiction. They emphasize the importance of finding the right support systems and treatment approaches, as well as the potential for personal growth and community impact in the process of recovery. Each narrative serves as a reminder that recovery is possible and that many individuals emerge stronger, more resilient, and committed to helping others in similar situations.

Beginning the journey of recovery can be overwhelming, but a wide array of programs, resources, and support networks exist to provide crucial guidance and encouragement. This section covers some of the most widely recognized support organizations, treatment programs, and tools for individuals and families affected by addiction.

Alcoholics Anonymous (AA) and Narcotics Anonymous (NA)

Founded in the 1930s, Alcoholics Anonymous (AA) has become one of the most recognized support organizations worldwide. Its foundational 12-step program emphasizes spiritual growth, self-reflection, and community. Members attend regular meetings, share experiences, and offer mutual support. Narcotics Anonymous

(NA) applies a similar structure, specifically tailored to individuals struggling with drug addiction. Both organizations are known for their inclusivity, accepting individuals at any stage of their recovery, and meetings are widely accessible in both urban and rural areas. NA and AA also provide literature, sponsorship networks, and online resources to accommodate members who may not be able to attend in person.

Celebrate Recovery

Celebrate Recovery combines Christian faith with the principles of the 12-step program, offering support for people overcoming addiction as well as other life challenges such as grief or relationship issues. Founded in 1991, Celebrate Recovery incorporates spiritual guidance and personal accountability, providing an alternative to those who seek a faith-based program. Meetings are hosted by churches across the country and have expanded internationally, providing a safe space for participants to discuss their struggles and personal journeys.

SMART Recovery (Self-Management and Recovery Training)

Unlike traditional 12-step programs, SMART Recovery offers a science-based approach to addiction recovery, focusing on cognitive behavioral therapy (CBT) and self-empowerment techniques. Meetings, both in person and online, teach tools for managing cravings, setting personal goals, and fostering emotional resilience. Participants learn practical skills such as problem-solving and relapse prevention, designed to help them regain control over their lives. SMART Recovery appeals to individuals who may prefer a secular program and offers extensive online resources, including worksheets and self-help tools.

Medication-Assisted Treatment (MAT)

For those struggling with opioid or alcohol dependence, medication-assisted treatment (MAT) can be a critical part of recovery. MAT combines FDA-approved medications like methadone, buprenorphine, or naltrexone with counseling and behavioral therapy. This approach aims to reduce withdrawal symptoms and cravings, allowing individuals to focus on recovery without the constant struggle against physical dependence. MAT programs are available in clinics, hospitals, and some private treatment centers, and are increasingly covered by health insurance and government assistance programs. However, MAT's effectiveness also depends on integrated care, where medication is supported by consistent therapeutic interventions.

Residential and Outpatient Rehabilitation Centers

Rehabilitation centers provide structured environments where individuals can focus intensively on their recovery. Residential rehab requires a commitment of time away from home, typically ranging from 30 to 90 days, and offers 24-hour support. These centers often use a combination of therapy methods, including individual counseling, group therapy, and holistic practices such as art therapy and physical fitness. Outpatient programs, by contrast, allow individuals to live at home while attending scheduled treatment sessions. Intensive outpatient programs (IOPs) offer flexibility and are often a viable option for those who cannot take time away from their daily responsibilities. Many treatment centers also incorporate family therapy and community re-integration planning to aid with long-term recovery.

Cognitive Behavioral Therapy (CBT) and Dialectical Behavior Therapy (DBT)

CBT and DBT are therapeutic methods often used in both individual and group therapy sessions to treat addiction and co-occurring mental health disorders. CBT focuses on identifying and changing patterns of thought that contribute to addictive behaviors, equipping individuals with tools to manage stress, cope with cravings, and prevent relapse. DBT builds on these principles and adds elements of mindfulness, emotional regulation, and acceptance techniques. Both therapies are accessible through outpatient programs, private practices, and increasingly via teletherapy, making them highly adaptable for different schedules and lifestyles.

Moral Reconation Therapy (MRT)

Moral Reconation Therapy (MRT) is an evidence-based, cognitive-behavioral treatment program designed to address antisocial behaviors often associated with addiction. Developed initially to help individuals in the criminal justice system, MRT has expanded to various settings, including addiction treatment. The therapy helps participants improve decision-making, develop moral reasoning, and increase personal responsibility, which is crucial for long-term recovery. MRT is often incorporated into group sessions, and its structured approach can be highly beneficial for individuals seeking to make lasting changes in behavior and mindset.

Online Support Networks and Apps

Technology has expanded access to recovery resources, allowing individuals to connect with support networks from anywhere. Mobile apps such as Sober Grid, I Am Sober, and Loosid provide social networks, accountability tools, and virtual support meetings, catering to different needs and preferences. Online communities and forums, like In the Rooms, offer a sense of camaraderie for those unable to attend in-person meetings. Virtual counseling platforms, including BetterHelp and Talkspace, make therapy more accessible, removing the logistical and financial barriers that often impede treatment.

Government and Community-Based Resources

Numerous government programs and community organizations provide accessible resources for addiction treatment and recovery. The Substance Abuse and Mental Health Services Administration (SAMHSA) operates a national helpline, connecting individuals with local treatment options, support groups, and crisis intervention services. Additionally, SAMHSA's Behavioral Health Treatment Services Locator is a valuable tool for finding nearby treatment providers. Community health centers, many of which receive government funding, also offer affordable or free services, including MAT, counseling, and recovery support, making them a vital resource for individuals who may not have private insurance or the means to afford private treatment.

Harm Reduction Programs

For individuals who are not ready or able to commit to full sobriety, harm reduction programs offer an alternative that prioritizes safety and health. Programs such as syringe exchange services, supervised consumption sites, and fentanyl testing provide immediate, practical assistance to reduce the risks associated with drug use. These programs do not necessarily aim for abstinence but instead focus on reducing overdose deaths, preventing the spread of infectious diseases, and connecting individuals with supportive services. Many community organizations and public health departments have adopted harm reduction approaches, recognizing them as an essential part of a comprehensive strategy to address addiction.

Family Support Programs

Addiction affects not only the individual but also their family, creating a need for resources that support loved ones through the recovery journey. Al-Anon and Nar-Anon are 12-step programs specifically designed for family members of individuals struggling with alcohol or drug addiction. These programs provide meetings, literature, and a supportive community to help families navigate the emotional challenges of addiction. Programs like Family Anonymous, SMART Family & Friends, and community-based family counseling services also provide resources for understanding addiction and establishing healthy boundaries, which can be crucial for both recovery and family cohesion.

Employment and Reintegration Programs

Job loss and financial instability are common side effects of addiction. Employment programs, such as those offered by The Salvation Army, Goodwill, and various government-funded initiatives, assist individuals in recovery by providing job training, resume-building workshops, and support for finding employment.

Reintegration programs, particularly those targeting individuals with criminal records related to substance use, help individuals transition back into society by offering mentorship, legal assistance, and life skills training.

Spiritual and Holistic Recovery Programs

For some, traditional treatments are complemented by a focus on spiritual or holistic healing practices. Programs like Refuge Recovery and Recovery Dharma, rooted in Buddhist principles, offer mindfulness-based approaches to recovery. Other holistic practices, such as yoga, acupuncture, and meditation, are increasingly integrated into rehab centers and outpatient programs. These practices address the physical, emotional, and spiritual dimensions of addiction, promoting balance and self-awareness.

This overview covers a variety of pathways that support different stages and preferences in the recovery process. From traditional 12-step programs to cutting-edge behavioral therapies and harm reduction strategies, these resources demonstrate that recovery is both a personal journey and a collaborative effort. For many, a combination of these resources offers the best support, providing diverse methods to meet the complex, multi-layered challenges of addiction recovery.

Government and Public Health Responses

The role of government and public health agencies in addressing the addiction and overdose crisis has evolved into one of the most significant public health missions of our time. In recent years, the scale of the crisis has pushed local, state, and federal bodies to rethink, expand, and innovate in their responses, creating new policies, resources, and collaborations to address the complexities of substance abuse. This chapter will examine these varied responses, from harm reduction and prevention initiatives to legislation and public awareness campaigns. It also delves into the challenges and criticisms faced by these programs and the evolving strategies public health experts and policymakers are employing to reduce addiction's impact.

Public health responses, like naloxone distribution, supervised consumption sites, and educational campaigns, work alongside policy shifts such as sentencing reform and the expansion of Medicaid coverage for addiction treatment. However, despite progress, barriers like limited funding, stigma, and jurisdictional constraints continue to impede comprehensive solutions. This chapter will explore these responses' scope, effectiveness, and limitations, providing a deeper understanding of the role and responsibility of government and public health agencies in combating one of the most pervasive health crises today.

In the United States, government policies aimed at combating drug use and trafficking have gone through significant changes, with varied levels of effectiveness. The Controlled Substances Act of 1970 established drug classifications, or schedules, intended to regulate and restrict drugs based on their medical use and potential for abuse. This legislation laid the foundation for drug policy, though critics argue that it contributed to stigmatizing addiction rather than providing support. By the 1980s, the Reagan administration's "War on Drugs" took a hardline, enforcement-heavy approach, leading to the criminalization of drug possession, especially targeting low-income communities and people of color. Mandatory minimum sentencing laws for drug offenses removed judicial discretion, resulting in widespread incarceration that disproportionately impacted marginalized populations.

Although the "War on Drugs" initially aimed to deter drug use and trafficking, evidence suggests that it largely failed to reduce addiction rates and placed an immense strain on the criminal justice system. Drug arrests soared, but addiction and overdose rates remained high, with few options for those struggling with substance use to access treatment. This punitive model received substantial criticism from public health officials, who emphasized the need for treatment over incarceration. In response, recent years have seen a gradual shift toward policies recognizing addiction as a health issue rather than solely a criminal one.

The opioid epidemic, which began in the 1990s, accelerated the urgency for policy reform. The Comprehensive Addiction and Recovery Act (CARA) of 2016 represented a significant shift, authorizing funding for prevention, treatment, and recovery programs. CARA focused on expanding access to naloxone, a life-saving overdose-reversal medication, and increasing treatment options, including medication-assisted treatment (MAT). However, while CARA was a positive step, advocates argued that it did not receive sufficient funding to address the full scale of the crisis.

More recently, harm reduction policies have gained traction as an effective approach to reducing overdose deaths and improving public health. Harm reduction includes programs such as syringe exchange services, supervised injection sites, and the distribution of fentanyl test strips to reduce the risk of overdose from contaminated drugs. These programs have shown effectiveness in lowering transmission rates of infectious diseases, like HIV and hepatitis, and in reducing overdose deaths. Nevertheless, harm reduction policies face opposition from some local and state governments, often due to stigma or a belief that such programs encourage drug use.

The Affordable Care Act (ACA) has also influenced addiction treatment by expanding Medicaid coverage, allowing more low-income individuals to access substance use disorder treatment. Medicaid expansion has been particularly impactful in states that opted to implement it, as it includes coverage for MAT and other treatment services. This expanded access to care is critical, yet gaps in service availability, particularly in rural areas, remain a challenge. Some states have additional restrictions or requirements that can limit access to treatment, despite the ACA's provisions.

At the federal level, recent administrations have continued to address addiction through funding for treatment and prevention programs. The SUPPORT for Patients and Communities Act of 2018 focused on curbing the opioid epidemic through expanded MAT access, prescription monitoring programs, and support for addiction research. However, many states face challenges implementing these programs due to limited resources and healthcare provider shortages.

Public health campaigns have also played an essential role in government policy, aiming to change public perceptions of addiction and raise awareness about the risks of opioids and other drugs. Campaigns like "Real Stories" by the Centers for Disease Control and Prevention (CDC) share the personal accounts of people affected by addiction, working to reduce stigma and promote understanding of substance use disorder as a health condition.

Despite these efforts, the effectiveness of government policies is often hindered by inconsistent funding, political divisions, and regional disparities in implementation. Some states and cities, such as Oregon and certain parts of California, have adopted policies decriminalizing the possession of small amounts of drugs in an effort to reduce the stigma of addiction and prioritize treatment over criminal charges. Yet, these approaches remain controversial, facing criticism from those who believe decriminalization may encourage drug use and from those who argue these measures alone do not provide sufficient support for recovery.

Overall, while there has been significant progress in rethinking drug policies, particularly around the opioid epidemic, challenges remain in achieving a unified and adequately funded response to the addiction crisis. Addressing these issues requires ongoing collaboration between local, state, and federal governments, as well as partnerships with community organizations and healthcare providers.

Harm reduction strategies focus on minimizing the health risks associated with drug use rather than attempting to eliminate drug use entirely. This public health approach has gained traction as overdose deaths rise, particularly those involving potent synthetic opioids like fentanyl. By prioritizing safety and reducing harm to individuals and communities, harm reduction methods like needle exchange programs, safe injection sites, and Narcan (naloxone) distribution aim to prevent infections, reduce the risk of overdose, and connect individuals to treatment options.

One of the most effective tools in harm reduction is Narcan, a brand name for naloxone, which can reverse opioid overdoses by quickly binding to opioid receptors and blocking the effects of opioids. Administered as an intranasal spray or injection, Narcan has become essential in saving lives amid the opioid crisis. Increasing access to Narcan, especially among first responders, family members, and even those who use opioids, is seen as a critical step in addressing rising overdose deaths. Studies have shown that Narcan's quick action can reverse the effects of an overdose within minutes, often giving individuals a second chance to seek help and pursue recovery.

Needle exchange programs, another harm reduction method, provide sterile syringes to individuals who inject drugs, thereby reducing the spread of bloodborne diseases such as HIV and hepatitis C. These programs, which may also offer disposal services for used needles, aim to create a safer environment for people who use drugs while reducing the public health risks of improperly discarded needles. In addition to providing clean syringes, many needle exchange programs offer other critical health services, including testing for infectious diseases, referrals to treatment, and access to naloxone. By reaching individuals who may be excluded from traditional healthcare systems, needle exchanges play a dual role in preventing disease and building pathways to recovery.

Safe injection sites, also known as supervised consumption sites, provide individuals a space to use drugs under medical supervision, significantly reducing the risk of overdose. These sites typically offer sterile equipment, medical support, and access to emergency care, as well as resources for treatment and social services. Countries such as Canada and parts of Europe have successfully implemented supervised injection sites, noting reductions in overdose fatalities and improvements in public safety. In the United States, the adoption of these sites has been slower, though cities like New York and Philadelphia have begun exploring the option.

Safe injection sites and needle exchanges are supported by studies showing harm reduction programs improve public health by reducing overdose rates and increasing access to medical resources. Safe injection sites, or supervised consumption facilities, have operated successfully in places like Vancouver, Canada, where Insite, North America's first government-sanctioned supervised injection site, has led to declines in overdose deaths and infections while connecting more people to recovery resources. Insite's model includes on-site staff who can administer naloxone in the event of an overdose, offer access to clean supplies, and refer clients to health and social services, helping bridge a gap that traditional health systems often fail to fill. This integration into the community has prompted calls for similar sites in U.S. cities, although there are legal and logistical barriers.

Narcan distribution plays a prominent role in overdose prevention and is now part of many harm reduction programs. Narcan's ease of use and rapid action in emergency situations have made it a critical tool for first responders and family members. Some U.S. states and cities have implemented laws to expand access, allowing anyone to obtain Narcan from a pharmacy without a prescription, making it more accessible. Additionally, nonprofit organizations and health departments distribute Narcan kits for free, often alongside education on recognizing overdose symptoms and safely administering the drug. The importance of Narcan cannot be overstated, as it provides immediate life-saving effects that often buy critical time for individuals to get emergency help.

However, despite the benefits, harm reduction strategies face challenges due to legal, political, and societal barriers. In some regions, harm reduction approaches face opposition from community members concerned about perceived encouragement of drug use. Critics of safe injection sites argue that they implicitly condone drug use and worry they may increase criminal activity. Proponents argue that these sites do not encourage drug use but instead prioritize safety, reduce disease spread, and provide a bridge to treatment for users who may otherwise remain isolated.

In addition to reducing overdose deaths, harm reduction programs aim to lessen the stigma around addiction, recognizing it as a public health issue rather than a moral failing. Programs like needle exchanges and supervised consumption sites bring people who use drugs into contact with health professionals, reducing stigma and potentially fostering trust that makes them more likely to seek help. Many programs also offer counseling and resources on-site, improving chances for engagement in longer-term treatment. By addressing addiction in a nonjudgmental way, these programs show that harm reduction is an approach based on compassion and practicality.

Another aspect of harm reduction is fentanyl test strip distribution, helping people detect fentanyl in other substances. Fentanyl, due to its extreme potency, poses a high risk when unknowingly mixed with other drugs like heroin or cocaine, significantly increasing overdose risks. Test strips allow people to check for fentanyl, empowering them to make safer choices, which can be particularly valuable in preventing accidental overdoses. Programs distributing fentanyl test strips have been praised as an essential harm reduction measure, offering another layer of safety for those at risk.

Moreover, these programs often work in conjunction with rehabilitation and recovery initiatives, providing pathways for individuals ready to begin the recovery process. Some harm reduction facilities offer connections to counseling, Medication-Assisted Treatment (MAT), and other recovery services. By integrating these options, harm reduction not only addresses immediate health risks but also connects individuals to resources for long-term change.

The healthcare system, nonprofit organizations, and community programs all play crucial roles in combating addiction and addressing the overdose crisis through prevention, treatment, and recovery support. Each brings unique strengths, working at various levels to create a network of support to tackle both the immediate effects and long-term challenges of addiction. These entities collaborate to address the underlying causes of addiction, promote harm reduction, and offer ongoing support for individuals and families affected by substance use disorders.

The healthcare system stands at the frontline in addressing addiction, largely through clinical treatment, emergency intervention, and preventative care. Hospitals, clinics, and primary care providers serve as initial contact points where individuals may seek help or receive addiction-related care. Healthcare providers assess, diagnose, and treat patients with addiction, often beginning with detoxification and medical stabilization. Detox is frequently the first step for individuals suffering from withdrawal symptoms, but ongoing treatment is essential to sustain recovery. Many hospitals and clinics have begun integrating specialized addiction services, including Medication-Assisted Treatment (MAT), which combines FDA-approved medications like methadone, buprenorphine, or naltrexone with counseling and behavioral therapies. MAT has proven highly effective in treating opioid addiction by reducing cravings, lowering the risk of overdose, and supporting individuals in regaining stability.

Healthcare providers also engage in harm reduction practices, such as prescribing naloxone and training patients and families on its use. Emergency departments often serve as critical intervention points, particularly for individuals experiencing overdoses. Beyond immediate care, providers increasingly use these moments to connect patients to ongoing support and treatment. Some hospitals have begun implementing "warm handoff" programs, where individuals treated for overdose or withdrawal are directly referred to addiction specialists or community-based resources, ensuring a continuum of care beyond the hospital. These interventions aim to bridge the gap between crisis care and long-term treatment, capitalizing on critical moments of contact.

Nonprofit organizations have historically been at the forefront of addressing addiction, filling gaps in services that might otherwise be inaccessible due to barriers like cost or availability. Nonprofits such as the Substance Abuse and Mental Health Services Administration (SAMHSA) provide educational resources, funding, and grants to community-based organizations working to combat addiction. Many local nonprofits operate recovery centers, offer peer counseling, and organize group meetings such as Alcoholics Anonymous (AA) or Narcotics Anonymous (NA), which provide essential support networks. Programs like Celebrate Recovery blend traditional group support with spirituality, catering to individuals seeking a faith-based approach. Nonprofits also play a significant role in harm reduction efforts, distributing naloxone kits, fentanyl test strips, and clean syringes to mitigate health risks associated with drug use.

These organizations often provide critical services to underserved populations, including homeless individuals, those without insurance, and individuals in rural areas where healthcare access may be limited. By offering free or low-cost services, nonprofits make it possible for people to access care regardless of their financial or social situation. Many also provide legal assistance, housing support, and employment counseling, recognizing that stable housing, employment, and legal support are integral to recovery.

Community programs often integrate healthcare, education, and social services to address the broader impact of addiction on families and neighborhoods. Programs led by community health centers frequently offer family counseling, parenting classes, and educational workshops to help those affected by a loved one's addiction. Community outreach programs also focus on youth prevention efforts, aiming to educate young people on the risks of substance use. This holistic approach addresses both individual needs and the broader social factors contributing to addiction.

Community-based harm reduction initiatives have become increasingly prevalent in recent years, as local organizations distribute naloxone, conduct safe syringe exchanges, and provide mobile health units for addiction treatment. Many of these programs rely on partnerships with local law enforcement, healthcare providers, and schools, creating networks that engage individuals across different stages of addiction. Law enforcement, for instance, is increasingly involved in diversion programs where individuals arrested for drug-related crimes are directed to treatment programs rather than incarcerated. Such collaborative approaches not only alleviate pressure on the justice system but also improve the chances of rehabilitation and reintegration into the community.

Public health departments also play a pivotal role by funding harm reduction services, organizing public awareness campaigns, and conducting research on addiction trends and treatment efficacy. At the state and local levels, health departments fund initiatives to distribute Narcan, promote syringe exchanges, and develop outreach programs for at-risk populations. These efforts are vital in shaping policies that reduce stigma and improve access to care.

Responses to the addiction and overdose crisis encompass a wide array of strategies aimed at reducing harm, improving health outcomes, and fostering recovery in affected communities. These strategies include government policies, public health initiatives, and community-driven programs that work collaboratively to address the multifaceted nature of substance use disorders.

Harm reduction approaches are integral to these efforts, with initiatives such as needle exchange programs and naloxone distribution playing a significant role in preventing overdose deaths and the spread of infectious diseases. Needle exchange programs provide clean needles to individuals who inject drugs, significantly reducing the transmission of HIV and hepatitis. Additionally, the distribution of naloxone, commonly known as Narcan, empowers individuals and bystanders to reverse opioid overdoses, saving countless lives.

The healthcare system also plays a vital role, with hospitals and community health organizations implementing protocols to support individuals struggling with addiction. Nonprofits contribute by offering resources, educational programs, and support networks that are essential for recovery. Together, these elements form a comprehensive approach to addressing the ongoing crisis, emphasizing the importance of accessibility and community involvement.

Information on available resources and programs can be found through health department websites, national organizations, and local community initiatives. These sources provide valuable insights into the programs and services designed to support individuals and families impacted by addiction.

Looking Forward – Solutions and Hope

The journey toward overcoming the addiction and overdose crisis in the United States is fraught with challenges, yet it is also filled with opportunities for meaningful change and recovery. As communities grapple with the devastating effects of substance use disorders, innovative solutions and a renewed commitment to compassion and understanding are emerging. The collective effort from individuals, families, healthcare providers, policymakers, and advocacy groups is essential to creating a future where recovery is not just possible but achievable for everyone affected by addiction.

Looking forward, there is a growing recognition that addressing the addiction crisis requires a holistic approach that encompasses prevention, treatment, and support. This chapter will explore effective strategies and emerging trends that hold promise for reducing the impact of addiction and overdose. From enhanced access to treatment options and harm reduction initiatives to increased community engagement and educational efforts, there is hope on the horizon. The power of resilience, coupled with a collaborative spirit, can drive the transformation needed to heal individuals and rebuild communities ravaged by addiction.

Addressing the addiction crisis requires holistic solutions that tackle the root causes of addiction and the associated criminal behavior. Substance use disorders are complex issues influenced by a myriad of factors, including socioeconomic conditions, mental health, trauma, and social environment. Effective strategies must go beyond treating the symptoms of addiction and instead focus on underlying issues that often lead individuals to substance use in the first place.

Research has shown that poverty and lack of access to education significantly contribute to higher rates of addiction. Communities with limited resources often lack adequate mental health services, job opportunities, and supportive social networks. For instance, the National Institute on Drug Abuse emphasizes the importance of socioeconomic status in shaping an individual's risk for substance abuse, suggesting that interventions should include improving economic opportunities and access to education .

Mental health plays a critical role in the onset of addiction. Many individuals struggling with substance use also face mental health disorders, such as depression and anxiety. Integrating mental health treatment with substance abuse programs can lead to better outcomes. For example, the Substance Abuse and Mental Health Services Administration (SAMHSA) promotes integrated care as a best practice, emphasizing the need for comprehensive treatment plans that address both mental health and addiction .

Trauma is another significant factor that drives individuals toward substance use. Experiences of abuse, neglect, or exposure to violence can create a cycle of addiction. Programs that focus on trauma-informed care have shown promise in helping individuals recover from addiction while addressing the psychological wounds that often accompany it. A study published in the Journal of Substance Abuse Treatment found that trauma-informed approaches improve treatment engagement and reduce relapse rates .

Community-based solutions are vital in creating supportive environments that foster recovery. Initiatives that engage local organizations, families, and individuals in prevention and treatment efforts can help build resilience and promote healthier lifestyles. For instance, community coalitions focused on prevention have been successful in reducing drug use among youth by providing education, resources, and support.

Addressing addiction also requires a shift in societal attitudes toward drug use and addiction. Stigmatization can prevent individuals from seeking help, perpetuating cycles of addiction and crime. Public education campaigns that promote understanding and compassion can help reduce stigma and encourage individuals to pursue treatment without fear of judgment.

Ultimately, holistic solutions to the addiction crisis must be comprehensive and multifaceted, combining prevention, education, treatment, and community support. By addressing the root causes of addiction, society can work toward breaking the cycles of substance abuse and crime, paving the way for healthier communities and improved outcomes for those affected by addiction.

The potential for policy reform, community engagement, and increased access to treatment is crucial for effectively addressing the growing addiction crisis in America. Many states have begun to recognize that traditional punitive approaches to drug use have not yielded positive outcomes. Instead, a focus on harm reduction strategies—such as needle exchange programs and supervised consumption sites—has shown promise in reducing overdose deaths and infectious diseases. For instance, countries that have decriminalized drug possession, like Portugal, have reported significant decreases in drug-related deaths and improvements in public health outcomes (Hughes & Stevens, 2010).

Community engagement is essential for developing tailored interventions that meet the specific needs of local populations. Organizations like the Community Anti-Drug Coalitions of America (CADCA) emphasize the importance of grassroots initiatives, working to educate the public, reduce stigma, and foster supportive environments for recovery. Local coalitions can mobilize resources and create action plans that address addiction comprehensively.

In addition, increasing access to treatment is paramount. While the Affordable Care Act has expanded insurance coverage for mental health and substance use disorders, many individuals still face barriers to accessing care. Telehealth services have emerged as a vital resource, particularly during the COVID-19 pandemic, by providing remote connections to treatment providers. Studies indicate that telehealth can improve access and engagement in addiction treatment, especially for individuals in rural areas or those with transportation challenges (Hwang et al., 2020).

Integrating addiction treatment into primary care settings can help normalize discussions about substance use. Healthcare providers equipped to screen for substance use disorders can facilitate early identification and intervention, leading to better outcomes. The Substance Abuse and Mental Health Services Administration (SAMHSA) offers training programs to support primary care providers in implementing effective screening and intervention protocols (SAMHSA, 2015).

Addressing the social determinants of health is another critical component of a holistic approach to addiction. Factors such as poverty, lack of education, and inadequate access to healthcare contribute significantly to individuals' risk of developing substance use disorders. Policy reforms focused on improving economic opportunities, enhancing education, and ensuring access to quality healthcare can create environments that support recovery.

Mental health awareness is integral to combating addiction. Many individuals with substance use disorders also experience co-occurring mental health conditions. By integrating mental health services with addiction treatment, healthcare systems can provide comprehensive care that improves recovery outcomes. Trauma-informed care approaches are particularly beneficial, as they help individuals address underlying issues that contribute to addiction.

Investing in community development initiatives is essential for fostering resilience. Programs that enhance infrastructure, provide affordable housing, and improve educational opportunities can reduce the prevalence of substance use by addressing the root causes of addiction. Research suggests that communities with strong social support networks and resources tend to have lower rates of substance use and addiction-related problems.

Ultimately, creating an effective response to the addiction crisis requires collaboration among various stakeholders. Policymakers, healthcare providers, community organizations, and individuals in recovery must work together to implement strategies that address both the symptoms and the underlying causes of addiction. By fostering a culture of support and understanding, communities can cultivate environments that encourage recovery and resilience while significantly reducing the impact of addiction on public health.

In the fight against the drug crisis, there are numerous stories of hope and progress that illuminate the resilience of individuals and communities facing addiction. These narratives not only inspire but also highlight effective approaches to recovery and the potential for meaningful change.

One poignant example is the story of Michael, a former opioid addict who found his path to recovery through a comprehensive treatment program that included medication-assisted treatment (MAT) and counseling. After years of struggling with addiction and facing numerous setbacks, Michael entered a recovery facility that provided a supportive environment and personalized care. Over time, he learned coping strategies, developed a strong support network, and embraced a lifestyle free from drugs. Today, he shares his story in schools and community centers, emphasizing the importance of seeking help and the effectiveness of recovery programs. His journey illustrates the transformative power of compassion and access to treatment, inspiring others to pursue their own recovery.

Similarly, the community of Silverton, Oregon, has made significant strides in combating addiction through innovative approaches. Local leaders implemented harm reduction strategies, including a needle exchange program and the distribution of Narcan, an opioid overdose reversal drug. These initiatives have not only reduced the number of overdoses but also fostered a sense of community responsibility and support. The success of these programs has led to increased engagement from local residents, who have come together to advocate for more resources and support services for those struggling with addiction. Their collective efforts underscore the impact that community involvement can have in addressing the drug crisis.

Another inspiring story comes from the city of Philadelphia, where grassroots organizations have mobilized to provide support for individuals affected by addiction. Programs like the "Philadelphia Resilience Project" focus on connecting individuals to recovery resources and mental health services while promoting a culture of acceptance and understanding. The project has successfully reached many individuals who previously felt isolated and stigmatized, empowering them to reclaim their lives. The stories of those who have benefited from such initiatives emphasize that recovery is not just possible but achievable with the right support.

In the realm of policy reform, states like Massachusetts have made significant progress in addressing the addiction crisis through comprehensive legislation aimed at expanding access to treatment and improving public health outcomes. The Massachusetts Overdose Prevention and Recovery Act has facilitated funding for various initiatives, including education programs, recovery housing, and job training for individuals in recovery. By prioritizing treatment over punishment, the state has seen a decrease in overdose rates, showcasing a model that other regions can adopt.

Additionally, organizations such as Alcoholics Anonymous (AA) and Narcotics Anonymous (NA) continue to play a vital role in supporting individuals in recovery. Many members of these programs have shared their personal journeys of overcoming addiction, emphasizing the sense of belonging and community that these support groups provide. Their shared experiences foster hope and remind others that they are not alone in their struggles.

Lastly, the ongoing work of nonprofits dedicated to addiction recovery, like Shatterproof and Faces & Voices of Recovery, highlights the importance of advocacy and awareness in the fight against the drug crisis. These organizations work tirelessly to dismantle stigma, promote policy changes, and create supportive environments for recovery. Their success stories reflect the collective effort required to combat addiction and the impact of community-driven initiatives.

These narratives of hope and progress serve as a powerful reminder that, while the addiction crisis remains a significant challenge, there are pathways to recovery and support. Each story, whether from individuals, communities, or organizations, contributes to a larger tapestry of resilience and strength in the face of adversity. By sharing these experiences and recognizing the progress made, society can foster a culture of hope and support for those affected by addiction.

In the fight against the drug crisis, there are numerous stories of hope and progress that illuminate the resilience of individuals and communities facing addiction. These narratives not only inspire but also highlight effective approaches to recovery and the potential for meaningful change.

One poignant example is the story of Michael, a former opioid addict who found his path to recovery through a comprehensive treatment program that included medication-assisted treatment (MAT) and counseling. After years of struggling with addiction and facing numerous setbacks, Michael entered a recovery facility that provided a supportive environment and personalized care. Over time, he learned coping strategies, developed a strong support network, and embraced a lifestyle free from drugs. Today, he shares his story in schools and community centers, emphasizing the importance of seeking help and the effectiveness of recovery programs. His journey illustrates the transformative power of compassion and access to treatment, inspiring others to pursue their own recovery.

Similarly, the community of Silverton, Oregon, has made significant strides in combating addiction through innovative approaches. Local leaders implemented harm reduction strategies, including a needle exchange program and the distribution of Narcan, an opioid overdose reversal drug. These initiatives have not only reduced the number of overdoses but also fostered a sense of community responsibility and support. The success of these programs has led to increased engagement from local residents, who have come together to advocate for more resources and support services for those struggling with addiction. Their collective efforts underscore the impact that community involvement can have in addressing the drug crisis.

Another inspiring story comes from the city of Philadelphia, where grassroots organizations have mobilized to provide support for individuals affected by addiction. Programs like the "Philadelphia Resilience Project" focus on connecting individuals to recovery resources and mental health services while promoting a culture of acceptance and understanding. The project has successfully reached many individuals who previously felt isolated and stigmatized, empowering them to reclaim their lives. The stories of those who have benefited from such initiatives emphasize that recovery is not just possible but achievable with the right support.

In the realm of policy reform, states like Massachusetts have made significant progress in addressing the addiction crisis through comprehensive legislation aimed at expanding access to treatment and improving public health outcomes. The Massachusetts Overdose

Prevention and Recovery Act has facilitated funding for various initiatives, including education programs, recovery housing, and job training for individuals in recovery. By prioritizing treatment over punishment, the state has seen a decrease in overdose rates, showcasing a model that other regions can adopt.

Additionally, organizations such as Alcoholics Anonymous (AA) and Narcotics Anonymous (NA) continue to play a vital role in supporting individuals in recovery. Many members of these programs have shared their personal journeys of overcoming addiction, emphasizing the sense of belonging and community that these support groups provide. Their shared experiences foster hope and remind others that they are not alone in their struggles.

Lastly, the ongoing work of nonprofits dedicated to addiction recovery, like Shatterproof and Faces & Voices of Recovery, highlights the importance of advocacy and awareness in the fight against the drug crisis. These organizations work tirelessly to dismantle stigma, promote policy changes, and create supportive environments for recovery. Their success stories reflect the collective effort required to combat addiction and the impact of community-driven initiatives.

These narratives of hope and progress serve as a powerful reminder that, while the addiction crisis remains a significant challenge, there are pathways to recovery and support. Each story, whether from individuals, communities, or organizations, contributes to a larger tapestry of resilience and strength in the face of adversity. By sharing these experiences and recognizing the progress made, society can foster a culture of hope and support for those affected by addiction.

In the ongoing battle against addiction, various organizations have emerged, providing essential support for individuals seeking treatment and sober living options. These entities focus on a holistic approach, addressing not just the addiction itself but also the accompanying social, economic, and psychological challenges that individuals face.

Here are some notable organizations making significant strides in this area:

1. Shatterproof: This national nonprofit is dedicated to reversing the addiction crisis in the U.S. by advocating for policy changes, providing resources for individuals and families affected by addiction, and promoting evidence-based treatment options. Shatterproof has developed a comprehensive recovery resource platform that connects individuals to treatment centers and support services. Their focus on destigmatizing addiction and promoting recovery makes them a vital player in the landscape of addiction treatment.

2. The Recovery Village: This organization operates multiple treatment facilities across the country, offering a range of services from detoxification to inpatient and outpatient rehab programs. The Recovery Village is known for its holistic approach, integrating therapy, counseling, and education about addiction. Their sober living programs provide individuals with a structured environment that fosters recovery and independence.

3. Facing Addiction with NCADD: Formed from a merger of the National Council on Alcoholism and Drug Dependence and Facing Addiction, this organization aims to create a national movement for prevention, treatment, and recovery support. They work with local communities to expand access to treatment and support systems, providing resources for families and individuals affected by addiction. Their focus on collaboration and community engagement has made a substantial impact on recovery efforts across the country.

4. Oxford House: This network of self-run, self-supported recovery houses offers sober living environments for individuals in recovery from substance use disorders. Each Oxford House operates under a democratic model where residents share responsibilities and support one another in their recovery journeys. With locations throughout the U.S., Oxford House has become a crucial resource for those seeking transitional housing.

5. Project HOME: Located in Philadelphia, Project HOME addresses homelessness and addiction through an integrated approach that combines housing, healthcare, and education. Their programs provide transitional housing and support services to individuals struggling with addiction, empowering them to achieve stability and long-term recovery. By focusing on the interconnected issues of homelessness and addiction, Project HOME has created a successful model for helping vulnerable populations.

6. The Salvation Army: With programs across the globe, The Salvation Army provides rehabilitation services for individuals battling addiction. Their Adult Rehabilitation Centers (ARCs) offer a faith-based recovery program that includes work therapy, counseling, and spiritual support. The Salvation Army's approach emphasizes the importance of community and personal transformation, helping individuals regain their footing and rebuild their lives.

7. The Hazelden Betty Ford Foundation: This organization is a leader in addiction treatment, providing comprehensive programs that include outpatient and inpatient care, sober living, and aftercare services. The foundation offers specialized programs for adolescents and adults, focusing on evidence-based practices that promote long-term recovery. Their commitment to education and advocacy also helps to raise awareness about addiction and its impact on families and communities.

8. Moral Reconation Therapy (MRT): While not an organization per se, MRT is a cognitive-behavioral therapy that has been effective in treating substance use disorders. Many treatment centers incorporate MRT into their programs, emphasizing personal responsibility and moral development. This therapeutic approach has shown promise in reducing recidivism and supporting individuals in recovery.

9. The National Alliance on Mental Illness (NAMI): NAMI offers support and resources for individuals dealing with mental health issues and addiction. Their programs provide education, advocacy, and peer

support, helping individuals navigate the complexities of treatment and recovery. By addressing the mental health aspects of addiction, NAMI plays a crucial role in fostering understanding and support.

10. Sober Living by the Sea: Based in California, this organization specializes in sober living environments that provide support for individuals transitioning from rehabilitation to independent living. Their facilities offer a range of programs, including outpatient therapy, life skills training, and community support, ensuring that individuals have the tools they need to maintain sobriety.

11. The Next Network: Based in Litchfield, IL, The Next Network is a nonprofit organization focused on providing support and resources for individuals recovering from addiction. They offer various programs that include peer support, life skills training, and connections to treatment services. By fostering a community of support, The Next Network aims to empower individuals to achieve lasting recovery and reintegrate into society successfully. I wanted to share my experience with this program because it genuinely saved my life. They didn't just offer help; they picked me up off the streets, gave me a safe place to stay while waiting for a detox bed, and got both me and my boyfriend into detox and rehab. Even now, they continue to support us on our journey. There are many other programs out there doing amazing work, but this one made a personal impact and gave me a real chance at a life in recovery. Shout out to those who work there Whitney Thomas Amanda Amanda Lauren Adrienne John and all the others!

These organizations exemplify the diverse approaches to addressing addiction, offering hope and pathways to recovery for those in need. By combining treatment with community support and advocacy, they are contributing to a growing movement aimed at tackling the addiction crisis and fostering resilience among individuals and families affected by substance use disorders.

Final Reflections

Looking back, the journey toward understanding addiction in this book has woven together complex and often deeply interlinked issues: from the biological grip of addiction to the economic, social, and emotional toll it takes on individuals, families, and communities. We've explored the roots and mechanisms of addiction, but also the powerful external influences that deepen the crisis, including the far-reaching impact of drug cartels and the deadly influx of substances like fentanyl. These organizations, driven by profit and power, exploit addiction and fuel an epidemic that destabilizes not only individual lives but also the very fabric of entire communities. The cartel involvement has heightened the stakes, bringing intense violence and creating sophisticated, harmful networks that intensify the addiction crisis across borders.

However, hope lies in the movement toward holistic solutions that recognize addiction as a multifaceted challenge needing coordinated care. As law enforcement battles these cartels, healthcare providers, community programs, and support networks also take on the responsibility of healing those affected. Sober living programs, nonprofits, and transitional housing, like The Next Network in Litchfield, Illinois, bring new opportunities for recovery, especially for those without access to immediate resources. Together, these approaches work in parallel to challenge both the direct forces of addiction and the systemic pressures that feed into it. With each step forward, the vision of a healthier, more resilient tomorrow becomes clearer.

As we conclude, the urgent call to action resonates deeply: we cannot combat this crisis in silos. Addiction, fueled by powerful forces like cartel-driven supply chains and societal barriers to treatment, requires a unified, sustained response from every sector of society. For readers, it means bringing awareness and compassion to the issue, advocating for evidence-based solutions, and supporting loved ones on their recovery paths. For policymakers, it's a responsibility to craft and fund initiatives that reach the underserved, prioritize harm reduction, and disrupt dangerous networks profiting from addiction.

Community leaders, healthcare providers, and local nonprofits stand as critical allies in this battle. Organizations like The Next Network have shown what's possible when dedication meets opportunity, illustrating that lives can be transformed even from the lowest points of addiction. We must expand these efforts, ensuring that more communities have access to effective, comprehensive support systems and that recovery resources are widely available and destigmatized.

Every action, from small steps to sweeping policy reforms, is a step toward a future where addiction no longer controls lives or devastates communities. The road ahead is challenging, but collective resolve, awareness, and sustained effort can make a difference. By coming together—individuals, communities, and institutions alike—we can address the multifaceted crisis of addiction and create pathways to healing, hope, and resilience.

References and Resources

1. Addiction and Recovery Research and Statistics
   •National Institute on Drug Abuse (NIDA) – The NIDA conducts essential research on addiction, offering up-to-date statistics, trends, and findings on substances and treatment methods in the U.S.
   Website: nida.nih.gov
   •Substance Abuse and Mental Health Services Administration (SAMHSA) – SAMHSA provides a wide range of research, resources, and a 24/7 National Helpline for treatment referrals and information on addiction and mental health support.
   Website: samhsa.gov
   •Centers for Disease Control and Prevention (CDC) – The CDC tracks data on overdose deaths, drug-related health issues, and the effectiveness of prevention efforts, offering extensive public health insights.
   Website: cdc.gov

2. Treatment Options and Resources
   •American Society of Addiction Medicine (ASAM) – ASAM provides resources for individuals seeking help and lists of certified addiction specialists for high-quality treatment.
   Website: asam.org
   •Detox and Rehab Directories – Sites like Rehabs.com and AddictionCenter.com provide nationwide directories of treatment centers, from detox programs to long-term rehabilitation facilities.
   Websites: rehabs.com, addictioncenter.com

3. Support and Community-Based Recovery Programs

- Alcoholics Anonymous (AA) and Narcotics Anonymous (NA) – These globally recognized 12-step programs support people recovering from alcohol and drug addiction through community groups and accountability.

Websites: aa.org, na.org

- Celebrate Recovery – A Christian-based recovery program that provides support for overcoming addiction and other life struggles through spiritual guidance.

Website: celebraterecovery.com

- SMART Recovery – A self-help program utilizing cognitive behavioral therapy techniques for those in recovery, focusing on self-empowerment.

Website: smartrecovery.org

4. Harm Reduction Resources

- Harm Reduction Coalition – An organization providing education and resources on harm reduction, including needle exchange programs and safe usage practices.

Website: harmreduction.org

- Narcan Resources – Many public health organizations offer Narcan (naloxone) training and free distribution programs to combat overdose deaths. Local health departments or pharmacies often provide access to naloxone.

- NEXT Distro – A mail-based service focused on harm reduction resources such as naloxone and syringe access.

Website: nextdistro.org

5. Educational and Advocacy Organizations

- Drug Policy Alliance (DPA) – Advocates for progressive drug policies and offers educational materials on harm reduction and decriminalization.

Website: drugpolicy.org

- Partnership to End Addiction – Focused on helping families understand and cope with addiction, offering online tools, counseling, and research.
Website: *drugfree.org*
- The Next Network (Litchfield, IL) – A nonprofit supporting individuals in recovery by connecting them with treatment resources, sober living options, and community support.
Website: *next-network.co*

6. Mental Health and Co-Occurring Disorders
- National Alliance on Mental Illness (NAMI) – NAMI provides support and information on mental health issues, including addiction and co-occurring disorders, through local chapters and online resources.
Website: *nami.org*
- Mental Health America (MHA) – Offers free online screenings, information on crisis support, and resources to connect individuals with mental health and addiction services.
Website: *mhanational.org*

7. Resources for Families and Children
- Al-Anon and Nar-Anon Family Groups – Support groups specifically for families of people with addiction, offering community and guidance.
Websites: *al-anon.org, nar-anon.org*
- Shatterproof – An organization aimed at ending the stigma surrounding addiction and improving access to treatment and resources.
Website: *shatterproof.org*

8. Community-Based Programs and Transitional Housing
- Oxford House – A nationwide network of democratically-run sober living homes that offer community support and affordable housing.
Website: *oxfordhouse.org*

- Kalimba Foundation – Another nationwide network of sober living homes that offer community support and affordable housing. I list this one because it's the one that I have been able to call home.
Website: kalimbahousecorp.com
- Transitional Housing Directories – For directories of halfway houses, sober living homes, and other transitional housing options, TransitionalHousing.org lists resources nationwide.
Website: transitionalhousing.org

9. Governmental and Policy-Focused Resources
- Office of National Drug Control Policy (ONDCP) – This office provides resources and information on U.S. drug policy initiatives and strategies for preventing addiction and overdose.
Website: whitehouse.gov/ondcp/
- DEA's National Prescription Drug Take Back Day – Offers guidance on safe prescription drug disposal to prevent misuse and environmental harm.
Website: dea.gov/takebackday

10. Educational Books and Documentaries
Books on Addiction and Recovery:

1. Love and Relationships: Building Relationships Beyond Addiction by Kaitlyn Doht – Explores rebuilding trust and connections beyond addiction's impact on relationships.

2. Pathways to Purpose: Thriving in Transitional Sober Living by Kaitlyn Doht – Provides insights into navigating the transitional living phase post-rehab.

3. Renewed Horizons: Embracing Life After Rehab by Kaitlyn Doht – Focuses on embracing a meaningful life after completing rehab.

4. Toward Tomorrow: A Sister's Guide to Navigating Addiction, Recovery, and Resilience by Kaitlyn Doht – A supportive resource for siblings and families affected by addiction.

5. In the Realm of Hungry Ghosts: Close Encounters with Addiction by Gabor Maté – A compassionate look into the psychology of addiction.

6. The Recovery Book: Answers to All Your Questions About Addiction and Alcoholism and Finding Health and Happiness in Sobriety by Al J. Mooney M.D. – A comprehensive guide for those recovering from substance use disorders.

7. Dopesick: Dealers, Doctors, and the Drug Company that Addicted America by Beth Macy – A critical examination of the opioid epidemic's history and its impact on communities.

- Documentaries and Films:

1. The Anonymous People (2013) – A documentary highlighting the recovery movement, focusing on individuals in long-term recovery and addressing the stigma of addiction.

2. Dopesick Nation (2018) – A Viceland series documenting two recovering addicts working in Florida's recovery community, showcasing the struggles of those trying to overcome opioid addiction.

3. Heroin(e) (2017) – This Oscar-nominated documentary follows three women—a fire chief, a judge, and a street

missionary—in Huntington, West Virginia, as they combat the opioid crisis on the front lines.

4.The Trade (2018) – A documentary series that gives an in-depth look into the drug trade, from cartel members in Mexico to addicts and law enforcement in the United States.

5.Recovery Boys (2018) – Directed by Elaine McMillion Sheldon, this documentary follows four men on a journey from addiction to recovery at a farm-based rehab facility in West Virginia.

6.Cartel Land (2015) – An intense look into Mexican and American vigilante groups fighting against drug cartels. This documentary captures the complexities and dangers of confronting the drug trade on the ground.

7.Ben Is Back (2018) – A drama film following a young man who unexpectedly returns home from rehab. His family's struggle highlights the personal toll addiction takes on loved ones and the challenges of recovery.

"The greatest glory in living lies not in never falling, but in rising every time we fall."
— Nelson Mandela

Also by Kaitlyn Doht

Renewed Horizons: Embracing Life After Rehab
Pathways to Purpose: Thriving in Transitional Sober Living
Love and Relationships Building Relationships Beyond Addiction
Toward Tomorrow: A Sister's Guide to Navigating Addiction, Recovery, and Resilience
Why Do I live with Mimi?
Understanding Health A Biopsychosocial Perspective
Beneath the Epidemic

About the Author

As a recovering addict who has battled meth and fentanyl addiction since the age of 25, I have faced numerous challenges and overdoses throughout my journey. My boyfriend, Matt, and I have struggled together on the path to recovery, enduring homelessness on the streets outside St. Louis—even in the freezing cold of winter. Had it not been for the amazing people who encouraged and supported us, we could still be on the streets or even dead. I believe God has kept me here for a purpose, and my mission is to share my experiences to help others on their path to recovery. By sharing my story, I hope to inspire and support those navigating similar struggles, guiding them toward healing and hope.

Milton Keynes UK
Ingram Content Group UK Ltd.
UKHW031214111124
451035UK00007B/721